'Jenny Rogers effectively invented the art of executive coaching, and she's certainly done more than anyone to advance and professionalize it. Her remarkable new book inhabits a place between fiction, non-fiction and memoir. It's *The Examined Life*, *Kitchen Table Wisdom*, *It's All in Your Head*, *Do No Harm*, *Love's Executioner* and *Let Me Not Be Mad* all rolled into one. It's a revealing look back on three decades of fascinating encounters, an honest examination of the big questions that make us all tick and, above all, a generous, wise and incredibly moving testament to the power of compassion, acceptance and change' Oliver Rawlins, Vice President of Communications, Netflix

'Jenny Rogers has done for coaching what Irving Yalom did for therapy: written a book full of moving stories that show the process and the benefits' John-Paul Flintoff, author of *A Modest Book About How to Give An Adequate Speech*

'Compelling and compassionate, comprehensive and challenging, the eighteen beautifully written client histories show that coaching is concerned with big questions of love, authenticity, self-worth, autonomy, isolation, life-purpose and death. Coaching is about listening with exquisite attention, offering acceptance, challenge and kindness' Dr John Raftery, former Vice Chancellor, London Metropolitan University

Are You Listening?

'Every coach and leader needs to read this book! F
engaging, impactful stories, *Are You Listening?* looks
curtain at coaching sessions with high level executiv
how to fuel your success with your failures and sha
struggles and triumphs of real leaders' Marshall Go
Thinkers 50 #1 Executive Coach and only two-tin
Leadership Thinker in the world

'Jenny Rogers cherishes the core of truth in each of us.
Listening? takes us with her as she brings people back
core. When you finish the book, you will see people diff
Not many gifts are for ever, but that one is'
Nancy Kline, bestselling author of
Time To Think

'*Are You Listening?* is quite simply the best book about coa
I have ever read. It's about the real experience of coach
rather than a new-and-improved template or method, so
right down to the tangled complexities of human exchar
growth. Jenny's wise and humane stories will make
better person' Sally Helgesen, author of
How Women Rise, The Female Advantage
and *The Web of Inclusion*

'Jenny's coaching was life-changing in my early ca
I have never forgotten her rare combination of att
rigour and wry humanity. Her beautifully writte
fascinating about the challenges of being humar
revelatory power of great coaching' Helen Boade
Director, BBC Radio

Are You Listening?

Stories from a Coaching Life

JENNY ROGERS

BUSINESS

PENGUIN BUSINESS

UK | USA | Canada | Ireland | Australia
India | New Zealand | South Africa

Penguin Business is part of the Penguin Random House group of companies
whose addresses can be found at global.penguinrandomhouse.com.

First published 2021
001

Typeset in 11/13 pt Dante MT Std
Typeset by Integra Software Services Pvt. Ltd, Pondicherry
Printed and bound in Great Britain by Clays Ltd, Elcograf S.p.A.

The authorized representative in the EEA is Penguin Random House Ireland,
Morrison Chambers, 32 Nassau Street, Dublin D02 YH68.

A CIP catalogue record for this book is available from the British Library

ISBN: 978-0-241-47464-8

Follow us on LinkedIn: https://www.linkedin.com/company/penguin-connect/

www.greenpenguin.co.uk

In Memory of Alan

Contents

Contents

Introduction

I have worked as a coach for three decades after earlier careers in teaching, television, publishing, management and consultancy. Mostly what I do is 'executive coaching', meaning that I work with people in senior roles and their organizations pay the bill. They come for two-hour sessions, typically every few weeks over an eight-month period or more. Sometimes I work with the same client for several years off and on and through a number of different jobs, so we get to know each other well.

Coaching is not therapy although therapy is a close cousin. My clients are mostly functioning well. If they have a mental health problem it will tend to be a minor one. If it is more than minor, and sometimes it is, then they need a different kind of help. The coaching I do, as with most executive coaches, is not about passing on my supposed wisdom through advice. If you rush to advise or rescue a client, you stop listening and you miss what you need to hear. Nor is it about being nice and nodding along to everything the client says. The art of coaching is to ask an astute question rather than to have a clever answer. Sometimes coaching is not about being nice at all because straight talking is what the client needs. Executive coaching is occasionally described as 'performance coaching' by the organizations who commission it, but that does the process an injustice. The whole person is always there and the rest of a client's life is always on the agenda one way or another.

My role is to provide a rare opportunity for people to be vulnerable, to talk through what is really bothering them, to know that there is no report-back to their organizations and that, unlike almost everyone else in their lives, I am suspending judgement.

It is an opportunity to take off the mask, to be seen as you really are without the stage clothes and disguises that most of us feel we have to adopt in order to protect ourselves. In doing this I am providing a quiet place where clients can look inwards as well as outwards, soberly assessing what matters to them and the decisions they need to make. My aim is that they will find acceptance that demands nothing in return. I describe this to them as being neutral but not neutered, unattached not detached, friendly but not a friend.

All coaching is about change. If nothing needs to change then you don't need a coach. But the bigger the change, and the more we know we need to embrace it, the more reluctant we can be to do so and the longer it takes. Fear is what holds us back. Clients could be in a successful career, but they may have suddenly lost their zest and have no idea where to go next. They may have been fired from a high-profile job and be the focus of press attacks or social media trolling. They may secretly wonder if they are good enough despite their appearance of uncrackable confidence. They may feel trapped in a failed marriage. They may be facing one of those dilemmas that involves a tempting offer where to accept would be to betray intensely held values. They may be nursing a secret which cannot be confessed because of its potential to humiliate and expose. They may have made a devastating mistake or have experienced a crushing disappointment while pretending to the rest of the world that everything is fine.

The foundation precept of coaching is that we have choice because we are responsible for ourselves. Other people cannot make us happy or unhappy. This idea can be terrifying, which perhaps is why some of us try to dissolve the oppressive anxiety it creates through addictions or by passing the responsibility for our well-being on to gods or demagogues. Few of my clients now have any religious faith but many start with the belief that what needs to change is other people, yet they discover through coaching that the only person you can ever reliably change is yourself – and that can be arduous.

Clients often begin by giving me what I think of as their 'cover story'. This is something safely small, usually to do with the surface discomforts of life in their organization, though it may be convincingly presented as urgent and important. A good example would be the many people who say they are overwhelmed by their work, there are too few hours in the day, they are appallingly busy, people pester them, they are obliged to deal with their emails even when they are on holiday. The cover story is part of what has helped the client function. It is what the psychologist Professor Franz Ruppert calls the 'survival self' and its job is to distract and protect. At some level the client is testing you: will you swallow the cover story? If you do, they may abandon the coaching, telling their friends and colleagues that you are useless. The real job of a coach is to enable the client to move from the cover story to the underlying story and to find a healthy way of answering the big questions that they may have been avoiding so skilfully for so long.

Where there are difficulties with the client's performance at work or in their relationships at home, coaching may be a way for people to move away from the labels so eagerly glued on to them by others. This labelling invariably implies that the labeller knows the other person's motivation and psychological make-up: allegedly they are *manipulative, attention seeking, lacking in self-esteem, bullies, neurotic, narcissistic* or, a popular phrase since autism became better known, *on the spectrum.* Most of us want to do well, we don't want opprobrium and failure. Yet, mysteriously, other people's instructions, criticisms, punishments and rewards have not shifted the challenging behaviour. In many cases it will have made it worse. A coach goes behind the symptom to ask, what problem is this behaviour designed to solve? When you ask this question, a different picture emerges, sometimes one where the client has never acquired the ability to manage frustration and disappointment or to learn how their behaviour strikes others. Sometimes they lack the vocabulary to put their feelings into words. With clients like this, the coaching approach is to identify such underlying deficits in skill and to work collaboratively on finding the solutions. Often this will prove to be the first time that anyone has truly listened to them.

Coaching is not about interpreting dreams or doing an indepth analysis of childhood, though in most cases childhood has an important part to play in the issues that clients bring. Many of us grow up with the impression that we are somehow not 'enough': not good enough, not clever enough, not well-behaved enough, not grateful enough. Every week I hear stories of parents who were hypercritical, unreasonably demanding, bigoted, seriously ill, cool, depressed, perpetually angry, dismissive, neglectful, absent or overtly abusive. Some early readers of these stories expressed surprise that a dysfunctional childhood features in so many of them. Their underlying question was, 'Doesn't this kind of trauma wreck people's lives and yet almost all of your clients have successful careers?' This is to misunderstand what trauma is. It is not a single event such as may trigger post-traumatic stress disorder. A better definition is that it is the lasting effect of experiences that are – or feel – life-threatening, including attachment failures in very early life with a permanent impact on our neurophysiology. It doesn't go away over time. It might become more intense through being ignored or denied. We can have had traumatizing experiences without having an explicit memory of them. Where 'survival' behaviour involves exceptionally hard work and long hours as part of our approach to defending ourselves against pain, it can be directly associated with success at work.

The stories in this book reflect the big questions, the ones that clients bring again and again. *Do I dare to start a new life? What will I have to sacrifice if I do?* Many organizations demand rigid levels of compliance so to choose visible difference in behaviour or appearance can seem risky. Authenticity is a constant theme: *Can I be my real self? Can I be unconventional? Will people still respect me if I show them my less attractive sides?* Some people have had bad news through staff-feedback surveys. Their dread is that they may not be able to change radically enough or quickly enough: *I've discovered that my team are afraid of me so can I really learn how not to be a bully?* Some clients have striven to make fortunes and then find that money has lost its allure. They are adrift and their millions feel meaningless: *What's my purpose in life? What do I want my legacy to be?* Some are struggling with loss or grief which has never been resolved: *Can I ever get over what happened?* Their issues reflect the most profound human concerns, which I see as these repeating themes: love, authenticity and self-worth, autonomy, isolation, life purpose and death. Often several of these themes are present at once and they thread in and out of the stories in this book.

It may seem as if my typical executive client is some kind of special breed and that their problems and concerns are unlike the ones that 'ordinary' people experience. I have not found that this is the case; their problems are exactly the same – except it is possibly true that the more high-ranking the client, the more isolated and lonely they are likely to be. Alongside these senior people, I work with younger and much less prominent people. The context may be different, the roles and responsibilities different, but the same issues crop up repeatedly.

When you explore these questions, the coaching room can sometimes become its own theatre. A marriage unravels right in front of you; a shaming confession is made; a secret hugged for many years is disclosed; tears of wrenching anger and despair can take up the whole session. These are times where you and the client hold your breath because nothing is ever going to be the same again.

Even so, despite these dramas and revelations, it is a fast track to delusion for any coach to believe that some specific technique or magical intervention is the equivalent of a drug that will 'cure' the client. Nor is it the case that there is some single moment where absolutely everything is resolved. Most coaching involves hard work over many weeks or months where tiny steps, some of which may involve going backwards, are more likely than giant strides. My aim is to provide an open, warm, honest and supportive relationship with clients, but even after all this time, I still don't know what the special ingredient is for success and I have learnt to be content with my ignorance.

You cannot do good work as a coach without bringing your own whole self to it, just as you ask the client to do with you. In asking that, you open yourself to being influenced by the client as much as the client is influenced by you. This is not about having the sort of fragile ego that is constantly seeking the client's problems in order to solve your own, nor of basking in the warmth of their gratitude as a way of finding the affirmation which is otherwise missing in your life. But you do have to be as undefended as your client. You can't pose as invulnerable, above all the drama of human existence. As a client, it is hard to trust someone with your vulnerability unless you see some glimpse of it in the coach and know that you will not be judged for your imperfections. This is why coaching is not something you *do to* a client; you are working side by side with them, always. Surprisingly often the client brings an issue that has some immediate bearing on your own life, so how could you not be learning and growing along with them and in some cases learning from them?

Everything in this book has happened but never in the exact way the stories describe, so to that extent they are fiction. I have ruthlessly blended identities, narratives and details to protect confidentiality. But each is true to the dilemma or issue it explores because each is essentially about what happens when our hopes collide with harsh reality. Coaching is about listening with exquisite attention, offering acceptance, challenge and kindness.

Both coach and client are grappling with the dilemmas so well summed up by the German-American philosopher and theologian Paul Tillich when he wrote, 'The courage to be is the courage to accept oneself, in spite of being unacceptable.'

Starting Afresh

Are You Listening?

I was summoned to a so-called 'chemistry meeting' at the head-quarters building, a shabby place well past its best. The phrase 'chemistry meeting' says it all. Some mysterious alchemy is supposed to occur – or not – where on the basis of thirty minutes of stilted conversation, client and coach agree to like each other enough to start working together. It can feel like an audition, especially when you are relatively new to coaching, as I was at this time. We met on a dark November day in the sixth-floor board-room, most of its space taken up by a very large, very ugly, very shiny table. I remember being aware that my fingers were a little sweaty, betraying my nervousness by leaving small paw prints on its surface.

Elizabeth had been newly appointed to a role in a public sector organization. It was enlightened enough to realize that the first year in a new job can be a time of uncertainty and faltering. The new person typically discovers that the job takes at least some skills that they do not possess; the appointing organization discovers that the new hire is not the hoped-for perfect fit to the job. Coaching is one way to head off some familiar difficulties by exploring them with someone who has worked with many such people before.

The coaching was not a success. It petered out after four meet-ings. I never lost my feelings of discomfort in Elizabeth's pres-ence. She seemed distant, a little haughty, and the problems she brought to the sessions were safely small-scale.

Looking back, I guess I was, like so many new coaches, unfeas-ibly fixed on *techniques*, *goals*, *models*, *frameworks* and other ways of hiding my terror of running out of things to say or do with a client. I had yet to realize that in the end it is just you and the client talking. As an experienced coach you steadily discard techniques in favour of being yourself in front of the client and encouraging the client to do the same. I did not know how to do this at the time nor why it was so important.

Over the years I did more work in Elizabeth's organization and when she got promoted again, often heard others speak of their dealings with her, unaware that I knew her. They would praise her incisive intelligence at the same time as they expressed concern that she was remote, scary and unknowable. One such client told me that the standard way of referring to her was 'Queen Elizabeth of Siberia, surrounded by a few chosen courtiers'. Elizabeth became well respected in her sector and was admired for the skilful way she had shielded services to the most vulnerable of its user populations.

This was not enough to protect her from disaster as a squeeze on costs began to bite. People at the top of public sector organizations are now paid salaries that seem high – the comparison is always with the prime minister's salary. In reporting what the chief executives and directors of this hospital or that quango or some local authority earn, there is often indignant squawking in the press that the sum is '50 per cent higher [or whatever] than the PM gets'. The sour, vindictive tone of this debate intensified. Everyone who runs a public sector organization is peculiarly vulnerable to calls for punishment when it is discovered that safeguarding has failed because a child or vulnerable adult has died. The argument goes that no matter how much further down the system this has occurred, the person at the top is ultimately responsible. The press invariably shouts, 'Off with their head!'

What happens next will depend on how skilfully the executive concerned has been able to build successful relationships with the opinion formers, including politicians and the press. Governments are increasingly powerless to shape the economy when so much business is global and owned by multinationals from other countries. No wonder then that they have to give the impression of firm leadership by bearing down on the public sector, the one arena where they are able to insist. I have worked with many clients over the years who have vividly described the bullying tactics of various ministers of state, fearful of losing media support if they are less than bold in their dealings with those who appear to have let down sacred institutions like the NHS.

I knew that Elizabeth had moved into another role, this time as one of the senior team in a new organization, the result of a clumsy and unpopular merger. Stories began to appear in the local and national press about the alarming size of this organization's deficit, something that could not possibly have been predicted, averted or managed by the incoming team. A general election was looming and Elizabeth was unlucky enough to have as chairman someone with close personal and political links to the man who was then the secretary of state in the area of her organization's operation. With no warning, the chairman was on the phone suggesting that she should resign immediately. As she later described it to me, he made no attempt to disguise his view that this was a cynical move and that she was the human sacrifice which had to be made. She was promised that her pension would be protected and that a discreet financial settlement would be made. She resigned.

There is no way of knowing which clients will disappear for ever from your life and which might resurface. I took it without surprise when Elizabeth called me saying she would value some coaching. Often in her circumstances clients want to redesign their CV/résumé, get help with job interviews or reconsider more generally where their careers are heading.

'What's our agenda?' I asked.

'Not sure,' she replied. 'But I know there are things I need to get off my chest.'

Our session started at ten o'clock and finished at midday. For most of that time Elizabeth was crying as she described her humiliation, disappointment and anger. Although clients do often cry, I have never known a session where there were so many tears.

She told me of the day she had left her job when she was intercepted in the reception area by a burly guard.

'Excuse me, ma'am, but you can't go any further. I need your laptop, car keys and fob.'

A young emissary from the chairman's office appeared. He was unable to hide his embarrassment. 'Sorry about this, it's because of security issues. We need you to go and walk around for half an hour in the park over the road or something. We'll pack up your things.'

Elizabeth described stumbling into the dismal little park in heavy rain, wearing thin shoes, dazed. 'Did they really think I would wreck my hard drive or delete everything on the server? As if I would have a clue about how to do that! There's a cafe in the park and I think I bought some coffee, but, you know, I can't really remember. I felt I was sleepwalking.'

On her return, the awkward young man was waiting. He thrust a bulging black refuse sack into her arms.

Elizabeth could list everything that it contained. 'There was a dictionary, an exhibition catalogue from Tate Britain, some notebooks, pens, personal letters, family photographs, make-up, a hairbrush, a nail file, a woollen wrap and a precious little clay figure made by my brother – he's a sculptor – as a birthday present. Of course, it got broken.'

She quoted the young emissary: 'You need to go home now and we'll be in touch about meetings to talk through your settlement.'

'He scurried away,' Elizabeth said. 'I remember noticing that he had a bright red patch on each cheek. I knew he was hating every minute. I thought it was appalling that the chairman was too cowardly to do his own dirty work.'

No help was offered with the question of how she would transport the clumsily packed bag of her possessions. She ordered and paid for the taxi herself while the reception staff looked away.

Since the day when Elizabeth described this unfeeling behaviour to me, I have heard dozens of other examples, all from conscientious public servants chased out of their jobs on a whim – chairs, chief executives, finance directors – in local government, education or in the health service. There is not even the excuse that these brutal sackings were in the public interest. In some cases, there were spiteful negative briefings, intended to destroy the reputation of the person concerned. The true reason was always party political.

Despite the shock, Elizabeth wisely employed a lawyer to negotiate for her. This woman protected her from any further meetings with her former colleagues. A bland statement was agreed, an allegedly face-saving formula that would deceive no one, along with a confidentiality agreement guaranteeing her a large sum of money in return for her silence.

Elizabeth told me that her husband had been unemployed for many years as a result of a serious accident and that she was always fearful for his physical and emotional health. She told me about the difficulty of finding time and money for the two sets of frail parents, all four of whom needed round-the-clock care. She expressed her contempt for the betrayal she felt she had experienced from her colleagues, many of whom she had thought were friends, especially her chief executive. This man had stood by and done nothing to support her, despite knowing that all the allegations against her were false and obviously unfair. She railed at the injustice and coldness of her treatment. She cried bitterly as she described her feelings of helplessness. She mourned the destruction of friendships with people she had admired, all casually wrecked by a move so brazenly motivated by political expediency. She described how, because of all this, there was no one in her immediate circle who could be trusted with her feelings because either they were too fragile themselves or else too implicated in the events that had triggered the loss of her job.

It is unusual for one adult to break down comprehensively in front of another because there is so much pride and carefully cultivated self-image at stake. To cry as an adult is to temporarily lose control, appearing to revert to childlike dependency. Despite our talent for cruelty as a species, we have probably survived by having an equal talent for empathy and caring: how else would we rear children through the vulnerability of their long infancy and adolescence? When adults express such feelings of sadness it can be unbearable to the listener because it awakens the part of our own brain that experiences the same emotion. What often happens is that a crying person gets offered trite phrases such as 'time will heal', or well-meaning onlookers interrupt the story to say that they know how you feel. Or they agree that the persecutors are evil and that the event is disastrous. Or, trying to create support, they start saying that they have experienced something just like it – and look, it was okay in the end! Or, even worse, the experience triggers some parallel memory of the listener's own and all too soon the conversational roles are reversed and the upset person has to comfort the listener.

Mostly what we experience in these circumstances is pretend listening where the listener is going through the motions and waiting openly or covertly for their turn in the conversation. Often the listener desperately wants the sobbing person to stop because they find it so uncomfortable to watch. The human urge to do something, anything, to be helpful is overwhelming. Mostly these interventions are not at all helpful. Even handing someone a tissue can appear to be saying, 'Please stop crying.' If you do speak, the simplest words are best: 'Tell me what happened, I'm here to listen'; 'How can I help?'; 'I'm so sorry' – and meaning it. The question for the listener is this: *Can I sit with your pain without trying to make it go away? Can I stay present without*

16

*being overwhelmed myself because your feelings of pain, loss, disgrace
or heartache trigger my own?*

It is arrogant to think that we know what is good for a distressed person or to assume that our experience is similar or that
what worked for us or others will work for them. It is literally
impossible to know what they are experiencing, so to say 'I know
how you feel' is absurd. Nor can we know why they have chosen
us as spectators to their grief or how they feel at giving vent to it.

After many years of working with other people's tears at their
losses, humiliations and disappointments, and crying not a few
unstoppable tears in my own life, I have understood that unhurried listening is by far the best thing to do. The difficulty is that
the more strongly you feel rapport with the crying person, the
more intense become your own transferred feelings of helplessness and anxiety. When you can control this and just listen,
the other person feels heard and accepted at a profound level.
Recovery may become possible from that point. Often in such
circumstances we have no greater gift than patiently offering a
hundred per cent of our attention. I think of this as listening with
intent to hear, really hear. Words are a poor second best.

Elizabeth made no apology for her crying. She had prudently
brought her own tissues. Slowly, imperceptibly, it seemed she
had cried all that she needed. I had scarcely moved or spoken for
two hours. I was still there.

That session was a one-off. Despite offering Elizabeth the
chance to return at any time, she did not.

By the end of the next twelve months, yet another reorgani-
zation looked likely. The secretary of state held on to his seat in
Parliament but lost his job after a change of government. It was
some time before I saw any public reference to him.

Three years later I met Elizabeth again at an event where I was
the facilitator. The subject was how to manage one vital part of
a new policy whose implementation would have a radical impact

on certain services. She was a participant at the meeting in her role as a successful interim executive, specializing in high-profile 'turn-arounds' – organizations where there had been some public crisis resulting in the departure of one or more senior people. She sought me out at the first coffee interval.

'Thank you for your advice that time, it was fantastic,' she said, smiling.

I must have looked as startled as I felt. 'I don't think I gave you any advice,' I said.

'Yes, exactly,' she replied.

Absolution

Carl found me through my website, so he was already unusual. Buying coaching is not like looking for a book on Amazon or an impulsive search for a new sweater. It is a high-value purchase and often made after months of considering whether some simple alternative might not only be thousands of per cent cheaper but also just as effective. Most of us coaches tend to write the same meaningless prattle on our websites about how amazing we are, working as we do 'in partnership' or 'to release your inner resources', even though I have yet to find a client who comes for coaching asking to release their inner resources. Potential clients are sensible enough to realize that some personal discomfort might necessarily be involved, so this is another reason for a client to postpone, procrastinate and rethink. Most people base their choice of coach on at least some element of personal recommendation. It is only by persistent private questioning of a trusted colleague or friend that a potential client will find out what it is really like working with us and whether the reality lives up to our hype. But Carl had no such personal contact. He wanted anonymity, though I did not understand why this was until much later.

Carl's organization was widely agreed to have failed. After more than a year of adverse publicity, there was no way it could continue as it was. Carl had been part of a substantial cohort of people who had been, as the organization squeamishly put it, 'let go'. A parsimonious amount of coaching or 'outplacement' had been offered by the incoming saviours. Carl had rejected it. 'I wanted nothing to do with them, I didn't trust them an inch. I'd rather pay for myself and find my own coach.'

I asked what he wanted from our sessions. His reply was, 'I need advice on getting my CV together and I need help in finding ways of minimizing the damage by association with that organization.' Many people expect that one swift session will be enough to recraft their CVs, but if this is all they need then they could just as easily get help from a book or from one of the many excellent internet sites devoted to this subject. You can only write a compelling CV when you know what you want to say about yourself. You can only do that when you have taken a good hard look at who you are, which skills you want to bring into the foreground and what you want from the next part of your life. Then it is easy enough to be shown some formats, to tinker with the prose so that it avoids pomposity or over-informality, hits just the right note of relaxed authority and is tailored to a specific job.

When people lose their jobs, the emotions are raw. So much is pitilessly disrupted: pleasant routine, effortless friendships, money coming in regularly and at least some acknowledgement of your skills. When you are a senior executive, you may have had an impressive job title, a secure pension, private medical insurance and an enviable salary. You may have artlessly enjoyed your place in the hierarchy. Work can give the recognition that all human beings crave because so much of your identity can be bound up in it. When, as Carl did, you lose your job with callous suddenness, when you have a stay-at-home wife, young children, school fees to pay, a substantial mortgage and the deadly opprobrium attached to a publicly disgraced organization, you can feel crushed by anxiety. Your confidence is wrecked, yet you know you have to find another job as soon as possible.

Many people are only dimly aware that they had made a psychological as well as an actual contract with the organization and that the psychological contract was the one that mattered. Here, there is an unwritten and unspoken exchange of social and psychological expectations and obligations. As an employee, you give your time and expertise in return for a degree of security, trust and respect. When the organization slips into the red, when there is a hostile takeover, when people uncover wrongdoing, or are just fired, the sense of disillusion and betrayal can be overwhelming.

Carl felt all of this. He was furious with his chief executive, furious with the journalists who had scented and then uncovered the story. He was furious with his colleagues, furious that he had found himself so tarnished. Most of our first session was devoted to an oddly flat description of this fury. He never raised his voice; there were no angrily flushed cheeks. There was a puzzling discrepancy between the extremity of the words he was using and the unemotional way he said them. Anger can give a certain degree of heroic energy, but it also destroys perspective because an angry person cannot think clearly. You can become fixed in your fury, enjoying the drama, liking the way it positions you as a victim, perversely relishing the distance it creates between you and others.

The word 'humiliating' appeared frequently in Carl's description of his experience.

'I never thought this would happen to me, I've always thought that people who got fired had brought it on themselves, losers. Now I've been labelled as one of them. Yes, it's humiliating.'

I put it to Carl that there were several ways to deal with humiliation. Many people simply plough on, pretending it never happened. I have worked with some clients who were unable to be honest, even in the assured privacy of the coaching room. There was the client whose employer had told me unequivocally that the client had failed her probationary period and had been sacked, but the client insisted to me throughout our time together that she had decided to leave of her own accord. There are high costs associated with this as a tactic. The negative emotion has nowhere to go but inside, and may then emerge as depression, panic attacks or in physical symptoms such as raised blood pressure or mysterious gut problems and headaches.

Carl nodded as I described some of this. 'Yes, that's what I've been doing, pretending. If people ask, I think I look pretty composed, but inside I get angry, I think they're looking for gossip or patronizing me with their pity. Keeping up appearances is essential.'

I asked whether this had come at the cost of any of the symptoms I had described. Carl shrugged. 'I suppose so. I've had two or three migraines a week since all this happened, but I'm used to them. They come in clusters so it's not that unusual.'

I had noticed that Carl was immaculately dressed for our session in a business suit, formal shirt and silk tie, even though he had already told me that he had come straight from home and was planning to go straight back there after we had finished. His reply to my comment on this was, 'Yes, I wanted you to see that I still have some self-respect.'

Carl needed to name the powerful emotion he was feeling for what it was: shame. Shame goes beyond mere embarrassment. It is about dread of what others will think. It is invasive and it is secret. Much shame is nothing to do with actual wrongdoing. I have worked with clients who felt shame about being 'old' or because they had been diagnosed with cancer or because their accent was one commonly associated with poverty and lack of education. Others have felt shame about their sexual orientation, their skin colour or their height. Many of these clients had been putting strenuous effort into trying to conceal whatever the allegedly shameful fact was. The energy this took was often poisoning their lives because it involved being constantly alert to the danger of exposure. A gay client lied to his parents and never spoke at work about his partner. A woman whose family had been Roma immigrants from Hungary had given herself a Scottish name and told people she was 'Borders born and bred'. A man born with a disfigured foot did what he could to hide it with special footwear and made a point of never referring to it in public. These were all factors which provoked shame even though in every case they were beyond the control of the individual.

I asked Carl what it was that he felt most shame about.

His reply was, 'Everybody knowing I've lost my job. People associating me with that organization. People finding my name on the internet, even though I was just a bit-part player, and I know it's worse for a lot of my colleagues. The unfairness of it. Uncertainty. Losing status, being seen as a has-been.'

I commented that Carl had not addressed me directly but had talked to his feet throughout this statement.

'To take away its power, shame has to be confronted. Could you bring yourself to say all that while looking at me, do you think? I promise you that nothing terrible will happen. I'm not going to shriek with horror, drive you out of the room or condemn you for having those feelings.'

Carl gave a small smile, looked me full in the face for the first time, and our work could begin.

What is the best way of dealing successfully with heartbreaking shame? It is virtually always by taking the counter-intuitive route and opening ourselves to vulnerability, talking to the people closest to us about our feelings and asking for help. Carl had, at least tentatively, begun to do this through deciding to work with me.

He was eminently employable. His skills had cash value and his career had an unusually broad base in terms of sector. We can often overestimate how much notice a potential employer will take of some career blip. If you target an employer, knowing that you are a good fit, compose a powerful CV that shows you understand what they need and that, as far as your skills go, you have what they want, then it is much easier to find a new job than it may seem. You do need to be able to tell the story of your departure from the last job in a way that puts the best possible face on it, but this is easier to do in practice than it might seem in theory. All that is usually needed is a brief, dispassionate account of being caught up in events where you certainly played some part, but without blaming, self-excoriating or shouldering martyr-like responsibility for events which were virtually always generated corporately. Employers have short memories where scandal is concerned and are often prepared to back their own judgement rather than to follow the herd of public opinion.

Some people sink under the weight of their confusion and bewilderment when they are living through this between-jobs phase. They loll about in bed, eat and drink too much, lose connection with everything that has motivated them in the past. Despite the sense of dislocation, this can also be a time of creative renewal. Carl had already instinctively understood the value of this odd period of downtime and nodded in recognition when I described it to him.

'I'm a would-have-been potter,' he said, 'but I opted for an economics degree and easy money instead of the life of poverty that would have followed art school.' In the six months since losing his job he had successfully competed for a place on a rigorous part-time course in ceramics at a well-known London college. His hero was Grayson Perry, the distinguished artist and ceramicist. 'Using my hands takes away some of the dross from my thoughts,' he said. 'I can pound the clay and tell myself it's some of those people I despise. And I think about Grayson, cheekily cross-dressed as one of his alter egos, Claire, to receive the Turner Prize, and I think, bugger them, I don't care!'

On the surface, all of this was going swimmingly. Carl was a model client, talked knowledgeably about searching for a job and did his 'homework' diligently. He always turned up on time for our meetings. Soon enough he was on shortlists and it was clear he would find well-paid work once more. We agreed a session where the plan was to prepare for a specific job interview.

Carl arrived, briskly refusing the large cup of coffee with which we usually started our sessions.

'I haven't been totally open with you,' he said. 'I've wasted some of our time together. I'd already read your book on being made redundant and your one on how to write a CV so there was nothing much that was new to me in what we've already done, though I suppose it was useful as a reinforcement.'

Then, after a pause, 'I do want to get the benefit of your ideas about how to get through this interview because it's a job I really want, but there's something more important that I need from you.'

Shame and guilt are sometimes used as synonyms, but they are entirely different emotions. Shame is about dreading the condemnation of others. Guilt is an internal process. It is the voice of conscience and can feel unbearable. When we feel guilty we accept that we have caused harm. We can feel shame without feeling guilt, even where there is plenty to feel guilty about, but we cannot feel guilt without also feeling shame. This accounts for the less than half-hearted apologies that people, anonymous and famous alike, can make when caught out in some misdemeanour. They carefully apologize for having 'offended' people but not for the offence because they feel shame but no guilt.

Admitting guilt hurts. It hurts our sense of ourselves as decent people. It awakens memories of being punished as children and of being told we were 'bad'. We feel remorse, yet at the same time there can be a compulsive temptation to blame the person we have harmed. Blaming the victim for somehow allowing the offence to happen is a common defence against genuine remorse. Where hospitals have failed their patients, their bosses have frequently tried to shift the responsibility on to the ward staff rather than accepting that it is managers who create and control the cultures where such behaviour is tolerated. When the rape of hundreds of young girls by gangs of men in British towns was finally uncovered, it was revealed that the police and social services staff had blamed these vulnerable children rather than their abusers.

I asked Carl what it was that he needed from me.

'I know you're not a priest,' he said, 'so don't take this the wrong way, but I think I just need to confess.'

I nodded and waited.

Carl described how a woman in his team had come to him with detailed information about people and events that would later prove to be at the core of what was amiss in the organization. Martha was young, she was junior. Perhaps out of nervousness and inexperience, she had handled the conversation ineptly, accusing Carl of complicity. He had reacted angrily, telling her she was exaggerating, she must have a personal agenda, her own performance wasn't brilliant, she was wrong to accuse her seniors and betters, she should desist from talking about any of it because it was slander and she could be punished. Shortly afterwards she had applied for a promotion in another department. He had made sure, through a few words to a colleague, that she did not get the job. She had then taken several weeks off work with a stress-related illness, had been referred to an occupational health specialist and had been 'managed out' of the organization. None of this had ever come out in public. He had said nothing of it to any of his colleagues, nor to friends, nor even to his wife. In describing it to me I noticed that he was unable to resist the temptation to blame Martha, even if just a little. 'If she'd been less emotional in that meeting, I would probably have paid more attention.'

People sometimes think coaching, counselling or therapy are soft options where all that happens is that the practitioner agrees with the client and tells them how wonderful they are. In the part of my own work where I train and supervise other coaches, I see that almost all beginner coaches can quickly learn to create rapport and to sit unobtrusively through tears, disappointments and doubts. When you take this to an extreme, there is a perpetual temptation to rescue, to comfort and collude, and to agree with the client that it's all other people's fault, the client was just unlucky – and sometimes that *is* the case.

Disagreeing or raising some troubling question is far harder than just supporting and being compassionate. Few other people in the client's life will confront them without having some ulterior motive. They may want to feel superior, to protect themselves or to pay them back for some alleged insult. Coaches have to learn how to confront with respect, understanding that they are crossing an invisible social line, judging when it is the right moment to do so, because often it will not be.

There was no getting away from it: Carl's organization had made some serious mistakes. Carl had now told me just how much a part of it he had been. Yet in the conversations up until that point, we had concentrated on the safe, externally focused task of reworking his personal PR. I had not previously heard him talk about any aspect of what it was that he or his organization had done wrong. I had not considered that it was my job to raise this with him, not even mildly or in passing. The phrase 'punishment enough' was probably somewhere in my head as I had made this decision. It is not a coach's business to act as prosecutor or magistrate. But all the same, I had noticed that he had never once expressed any personal guilt and that even now he was seemingly unable to take full responsibility for his actions.

'So it was Martha's fault?' I asked mildly.

Carl stopped talking, then slowly shook his head. 'No, no, she was just a kid. It was wrong of me to say that. It was us. Me and my colleagues. We made the decisions, we created what happened.'

Guilt is a consequence of breaching a personal moral code. In saying this, I asked him which particular aspect of his own code he had ignored. The reply was that he, among the rest of the senior team, had espoused a set of values about transparency, honesty and the highest standards of service. His and their actions had violated all of them. Worse than that, he had acted with malice and had personally destroyed the career in the organization of that young woman in order to save his own skin.

'Moral cowardice of the worst order,' was his own verdict. For the first time his voice shook a little. 'If I'd taken a moment, if I'd thought it through, if I hadn't panicked, I might have been able to prevent the whole disaster from happening.'

I agreed briefly that he had indeed made a grave mistake, though whether he could single-handedly have stopped the rot, I doubted. If there is any organization that lives up to the values piously listed on its website, I have yet to meet it. Failing to act at all times according to your values is a condition of being alive; we all breach our values all the time and are then perpetually at risk of seeming like hypocrites. But at least by stating our values we aspire to better behaviour. As the French philosopher François de La Rochefoucauld said, 'Hypocrisy is the homage vice pays to virtue.' This hypocrisy had unravelled spectacularly in the case of Carl and his organization.

Though neither Carl nor I had any religious beliefs, we agreed that Christianity and Judaism know a thing or two about guilt. The most important event in the Jewish calendar of High Holy Days is Yom Kippur, the Day of Atonement, when you fast, pray, confess your faults, repent and vow to lead a better life.

'I've never done it myself,' I said, 'but going into a dark box in a Catholic church to confess your sins anonymously to a hidden listener who then doles out a penance, a symbolic punishment, often seems to leave the penitent feeling that they can start anew.'

Unlike shame, guilt gives energy for change because it asks, *What's the lesson here?* Carl said the underlying lesson for him was that in any future managerial role it would be essential to connect with junior staff, putting himself on occasional shifts with them, listening to them – and to understand how readily standards could slip. It would also be about speaking up and risking the possibility of suffering the fate – banishment and punishment – of so many whistle-blowers.

Then comes the hard part: self-forgiveness. I directed Carl to a website that lists daily mantras for self-forgiveness, including perhaps the most challenging one of all: *There is nothing, repeat nothing, that is too terrible to be forgiven.* These mantras also follow the Christian and Judaic traditions in pointing out that it is the sin that is wrong, not the sinner.

There is a high price to pay for being unable to forgive yourself. Unresolved remorse means living with self-inflicted hurt and pain. Negativity and pessimism become ingrained. The fear of repeating the mistake can be paralysing. Without forgiveness, self-loathing becomes a habit; you tell yourself you do not deserve compassion and that it is better to disappear as a way of making sure you never damage anyone again. This had been Carl's inner landscape, well hidden under his apparent insouciance.

'It may seem weird and self-defeating,' he said, 'but up until our first session, I hadn't applied for a single job, despite all my worries about money.'

Ninety minutes of discussion later, Carl left. I had several emails from him, some of them comically self-critical ('I can't even do this self-forgiveness thing properly') where he described practising in front of a mirror. The last one said, 'this time I managed to look at myself, so something must be changing'. The email ended with a question: 'Should I contact Martha to apologize?'

Making amends is a standard part of any Twelve Step programme, where recovering addicts are encouraged to write to or otherwise contact people they believe they may have harmed. This is remorse in action and it is also enshrined in formal processes such as the Truth and Reconciliation Commission, the monumental restorative justice body that was established in South Africa as the country emerged from the era of apartheid. The theory is that facing the person you have harmed means you face the consequences of your actions. It also gives the harmed person the chance to offer forgiveness, as much a healing process for them as for the perpetrator. Much can go wrong in practice. The person who was harmed may not believe the remorse is genuine, or if they do, may feel it would be too upsetting to meet or to have anything to do with the perpetrator. If there is a meeting, the victim may refuse to accept the apology, leaving the penitent unforgiven, possibly feeling worse than if no contact had been made. Sometimes there are legal or other barriers. A doctor client, whose mistake during surgery had left a patient permanently paralysed, was strongly advised by his insurer to avoid admitting guilt or apologizing, even though he was desperate to do so.

One option is to write a letter, which you may write and set aside, or send, depending on circumstances. Carl emailed me to say that he had chosen to draft a letter but not to send it. He did not attach the draft and I did not ask to read it.

It looked as if that was to be my last contact with him. He never returned for the session on how to get through a job interview successfully. Perhaps he had my book on that topic too, and my emails went unanswered.

At the time I was working with Carl I was struggling to come to terms with having made a shaming professional mistake. It was inadvertent, born out of carelessness, a degree of recklessness, bad luck, some egotism and overconfidence. My mistake could have been the cause of harm to the client concerned and I still don't know whether or not it was. I did meet the client. My explanation of the circumstances was heard with evident incredulity, my faltering apology received with frosty graciousness. The work was terminated immediately. So I, too, had been fired.

Although Carl's issue and my own had nothing in common in their context, the psychological impact was very similar. Like him, I was obsessively preoccupied with 'if only' thinking, wishing I could turn the clock back, endlessly wondering how I could have been so foolish. I was ruminating on the horror of it. I was taking complicated detours to avoid travelling through the part of London associated with my client's offices. It was hard to remind myself that nobody had died, and that a single mistake did not define me as a professional or as a human being. The reason I was able to refer Carl so readily to a useful website was that I had only recently consulted and learnt from it myself.

I had also discovered the healing power of confession. Coaches are strongly advised to have a supervisor, not someone who acts in the everyday meaning of the word but a fellow coach whom you engage on an ad hoc basis and whose role is to listen and comment dispassionately. Even though Jules and I knew each other well, I still trembled violently as I made the call to her. Would she now see me as a fatally flawed coach? Would she secretly or overtly judge me?

Jules received my confession impassively. She commented that in meeting and apologizing I had given my client back a degree of control. That the people who loved me were unlikely to be affected one way or the other by what had happened – my professional life was most likely a mystery to them anyway.

'At this point,' she said, 'you need to avoid becoming a victim yourself. You need to interrogate this episode, noting it, telling yourself, *I have paid attention and now it's time to move on*.'

Jules argued that I needed to do this in order, as she put it, to be *available*, emotionally and psychologically, for my clients. Like Carl, I had said nothing to my family or immediate colleagues. Jules recommended some confession-lite to those closest to me.

Why does confession work? The essence of the answer is that the confessor is unmoved by the shock or horror of whatever the sinner has done, yet acknowledges that it was wrong. The confessor does not brush aside the mistake with false reassurances. The confessor agrees that some mistakes have terrible consequences. The confessor does not reject or punish but accepts that being human means that we make mistakes. By doing this, the confessor gives absolution, whether or not words of absolution are spoken.

In following Jules's good advice, I forced myself to start a limited programme of describing what had happened with those I love and trust, choosing as my first hearer my husband, Alan, who, unknown to any of us, was entering the last year of his life. His unwavering Christian faith had often been a source of friction between us. He was baffled by what he saw as my obstinate refusal to see obvious spiritual truth. I was baffled by what seemed to me like superstition. Like Jules, he listened patiently. We were at our house in Norfolk. It was a warm Sunday morning at the height of summer and he trundled off to church in his powered wheelchair. He came back after the service and quickly tapped away at his computer.

'Here,' he said, 'we all chanted this as usual from the Book of Common Prayer and Damien [the parson] then said the responses and we all got beautifully forgiven for our sins. I thought you might like to go off somewhere into the garden – it's a sunny day – and chant it for yourself. God will hear, even if you don't think so.'

What he had typed and printed out read:

We acknowledge and bewail our manifold sins and wickedness which we from time to time most grievously have committed by thought word and deed against Thy divine majesty. We do earnestly repent and are heartily sorry for these, our misdoings; the remembrance of them is grievous unto us; the burden of them is intolerable. Have mercy on us, have mercy on us, most merciful Father. Forgive us all that is past. And grant that we may hereafter serve and please Thee in the newness of life.

I did go outside. Despite my dogged atheism, I recited this General Confession, versions of which have been part of Anglican services for many centuries, addressing the ancient oak tree dominating our garden and looking out over the field to the church which had been part of an unchanging landscape for a thousand years. I clung to that piece of paper until it became worn and soft with creases, and still have it. After Alan died, in the agony of bereavement I reread it many times as part of the inevitable regrets that most of us will have about whether we were always as unfailingly loving as we should have been to the person who has died.

After another two years of silence, I had an invitation from Carl to connect on LinkedIn. His profile described his current glossy job. I replied with a short message asking for an update. Back came, not words, but some beautifully photographed pictures. These were of a pot, using Grayson Perry's technique of embellishing a simple classical shape with pictures and text. The pot did not have any of the saucier graphics of the sort so mischievously created by Grayson, but just under its lip was a quote from Voltaire which read:

Everyone is guilty of all the good they did not do.

And then, at the base, a quote from the Dalai Lama:

If you don't have compassion for yourself, you can't have compassion for others.

The Empty Heart

I first met Hamish at a summer party. He was a cousin of Fiona, a client I was fond of and had worked with on and off for some years through a number of jobs and promotions. Our social circles overlapped and we sometimes met at such events. Hamish was hard to miss with his lanky six-foot-plus frame, bright-red hair and loud, confident voice.

Fiona introduced us.

'Oh yes,' he said, giving me a narrow-eyed look that suggested scepticism at best, hostility at worst. 'Fi's talked about you. You've obviously got her tamed right enough. You're one of those wee so-called coaches. I've read all about people like you in the *FT*.'

The former *Financial Times* columnist Lucy Kellaway is a relentless mocker of organizational nonsense. At the time she was writing a witty spoof on coaching as a faddish solution to management problems. It involved fictional emails between a nincompoop called Martin Lukes, director of marketing at the wonderfully and pretentiously named a-b glöbâl (UK), and his coach, Pandora. These columns later became a book called *Who Moved My BlackBerry?* Pandora spouts a mix of New Age baloney and half-digested, half-understood coaching 'techniques' at her credulous client. For instance, she suggests imagining a red rose and a white rose in each half of his brain and ends her every email with the words 'Strive and Thrive!' Far from advancing his career, Martin ends his year of 'coaching' from Pandora having lost his job and being shifted into the career graveyard of Special Projects.

I read this book alternately laughing out loud and cringing at the accuracy of its depiction of a particular type of coach who

34

has neither expertise in any subject nor any underpinning psychological insight. No coach reading the book could fail to ask how much they had in themselves of Pandora and CoachworX, her all-too-familiar-sounding company.

The sharpness of Hamish's words to a complete stranger and the swiftness of his attack surprised me as it seemed discourteous, not just to me but to his cousin too, and an inappropriate tone for a light-hearted social occasion. But I have developed a pretty good poker face over the years and I replied with some enthusiastic agreement about the *FT* column. I did not attempt to do what he clearly expected and wanted, which was to defend myself and my profession, thus provoking further debate.

Hamish wasn't giving up so easily. 'So people actually pay you money for this daft stuff, do they?'

'They do indeed,' I replied, by now thinking it was a little unnatural for him to have such a fierce interest in something he purported to find so risible. Simultaneously, I was starting to edge away. I reached into my bag. 'Here,' I said, 'have my card, and if you ever need a coach who's not like Pandora, give me a call.' I waved my glass in farewell and wheeled smartly away to the opposite corner of the large marquee.

I forgot him. I had so little interest that even when Fiona told me at our next session that she was embarrassed by what she called his 'typical Glaswegian fieriness' and said that he was a successful entrepreneur, I nodded politely and forgot him again.

A few years later I was eating my way through a quiet lunch between clients when my mobile rang with a number I did not recognize.

'Is that Jenny Rogers?'

'Yes,' I said. I was cautious, thinking that since it was not an 0800 number at least it was not a cold call from someone trying to sell me gas or electricity.

'I'm that rude Scottish fellow you met at Fiona's party. Will you talk to me if I humbly apologize?'

Hamish said he might or might not need something he called 'a bit of help'. When I asked what sort of help, he hedged. 'I'll tell you what it is if I decide to go ahead.'

I explained that *help* as such was a feeble word for coaching. Coaching is *work*, though both sides have to hope that the outcome of it is *helpful*, adding that I never assume I am the right coach for any particular individual or that coaching is the right solution for whatever it is that the potential client wants to tackle.

'Could I just have a trial session to see whether I like it?'

'You can stop at any time, as indeed I can, but it would be great to know what your agenda would be for the coaching, if we both decided it was the right thing for you.'

A long pause. And then, tersely, 'It's about what to do with the rest of my life.'

'That's a big question. What's brought it into focus right now?'

'I've sold my company. My personal life is a mess. Is that enough excuse for this coaching thing, d'you think?'

Paying attention to how clients conduct themselves in this conversation always yields data about them and points to how the relationship might develop. I noticed that despite a gracious apology for his previous behaviour, he was treating me as if I was a desperate salesperson on whom he might kindly bestow his custom, even though I had not solicited the contact and was making it plain that it was my choice as much as his about whether to take it to the next stage. This was clearer still when he asked about fees, expressed pantomime amazement at the answer, and instantly tried to negotiate a discount.

I was intrigued. I warmed to his combination of cockiness, raw humour and rough humility. I was amused by what seemed like an automatic attempt to talk down my perfectly reasonable fee, something that had been immediately preceded by shameless boasting about his wealth and telling me that he had no need to work. I recognized his approach-avoid tactics as just another version of how so many clients feel about taking on a coach. Most people do understand that for coaching to succeed they have to take the risk of being vulnerable, but we all become experts at protecting ourselves, hiding our weaknesses, dreading being exposed.

We agreed that we would work together.

At the first session I said, 'I asked you to think about the agenda we would be working on. How did you get on with that?'

'Couldn't do it really. Couldn't find the right words.' There was a brief silence, and then he said abruptly, 'You see, the real problem is that this is empty. Empty.' Hamish struck the left side of his chest so hard that I heard the thud. 'Yes, I have an empty heart, a hole where it should be.' He stared somewhere past my left shoulder. 'Can an empty heart be filled?'

Hamish expressed curiosity about people who were driven by the wish to do some social good, people who had some obvious vocation even if, as he said – and perhaps there was an implied put-down here – 'they earn poverty wages'. He asked me about other clients. I told him, personal details carefully concealed, about the doctor whose own chronic disease in childhood had led him away from lucrative private practice and into research which had helped develop a new drug for other sufferers from the same condition. Then there was the Anglican priest who had chosen an impoverished inner-city parish rather than a soft job in a prosperous suburb, the successful City trader who had retrained as a teacher, the senior NHS manager who had resigned in order to care full-time for his terminally ill wife.

'I envy them,' said Hamish.

'What do you envy?'

'They're free from the compulsion to make and spend money.'

'You don't know that they are,' I said. 'I'm just telling you what their purpose or vocations are, it doesn't mean they never feel envious of people who have more money.'

'Yes, but they will die knowing they have made a difference. At the moment, what can I say? I haven't, it's all been about me, me, me; me, myself and I.'

Hamish told me that he had been adopted at a few days old and was to be his parents' only child. It was a 'closed' adoption, meaning that his birth mother gave up any right to maintain contact. There was little money but he had been cherished, indulged, adored. The story of his adoption had seemingly been as well handled as it was possible to do, with an emphasis on how he had been 'chosen'. School had at first been effortless. He had excelled academically and at sport. At sixteen he had done what he described as 'getting in with the wrong crowd'. There was experimenting with drugs, hanging out with a gang of boys from less stable homes, truanting, some police cautions and a precipitous slide in schoolwork. The trigger seemed to have been other boys teasing him about his red hair and then taunting him about his adoption. At seventeen, after some unimpressive exam results, he left school to work in a car repair business. No one, not teachers, not parents, nor other family, could reach him.

'I was out of control,' he said, 'I disappointed everyone. My dad was so bitter he said I'd never amount to anything. He more or less told me he regretted taking me in. My mum just cried every time I saw her.'

At nineteen his luck turned. Through his work he met the owner of a local taxi fleet. This man expressed his belief that Hamish had talent and potential, acted as an informal mentor and did not condemn him for any of his previous behaviour while making it clear that it had been foolish. Within a few months Hamish enrolled at his local college, won a place on an engineering course at a good university and restored communication with his parents.

From an original interest in mechanics, 'because machines don't let you down like humans do', he moved to electronics. He said he was clear from his early twenties that he never wanted to work for anyone else and that he would create his own business. His entrepreneurial career had started early. At twenty he had seen a man selling copies of designer watches in a pub, had impulsively bought the entire tray and had then sold them within a few days to his fellow students at a 200 per cent profit. Starting from a shaky base where the question was survival, Hamish had built a successful business. He had now sold the company for many millions and was free of any commitment to its future. Within the same year his second marriage had ended.

I asked what was behind the decision to sell his company.

'I was bored with it, bored, bored, bored. Everything was coming round for the umpteenth time. I'd savaged my competitors, proved my dad wrong, proved that I could amount to something – in fact, with a few more millions I could amount to enough to be in one of those Rich Lists!' Hamish looked hard at me as he delivered this last sentence.

I assumed that I was meant to be impressed, and I was. I told Hamish that I understood how much effort, ingenuity and managerial competence it takes to build such a successful company. Virtually all small companies fail to grow to this level. Their owners succumb to innumerable problems en route. They can't delegate, they mismanage their cash flow, their ability to innovate fails to keep up with what the market needs, they hire the wrong people. As I was saying this and saw Hamish's unexpectedly blank face, I realized I had probably missed the point. It was the lure of the Rich List that was the point, not his skill in building a business.

'It's being in the Rich List that you would be most proud of?'

'Well, yes, wouldn't you be? If there was a list of the World's Best Coaches, would you be good enough to be on it?'

In his life story I noticed the language of violence, war and competition. He had *forced down* the price asked by the watch seller, he had *slammed into* or *killed* competitors, he had *beaten the living daylights* out of the *train crash* companies he had acquired who had had the nerve to ask *nuclear* prices for distressed assets. He had *driven a tank through them*, getting *knock-down* prices, making it possible to resell their assets with a huge profit as the *spoils of victory*. He had *trounced* the opposition in the *race* to be first and best.

Drawing attention to all these metaphors, I said, 'So, Hamish, it seems that everything is a war or a competition. And it's one you have to win?'

Human motivation is one of the most studied topics in psychology. *Intrinsic* motivation is powerful. It is what we feel when we gratify our need to grow, to develop, to reach our potential. It is about the satisfaction of effort; it is what is involved when we try hard without anyone having to spur us on. *Extrinsic* motivation is more fragile because it is about reward bestowed by others: prizes, medals, the office with two sets of windows, a bigger salary – and appearing in a newspaper list of very rich people. It creates insecurity because we all know that it can be snatched away at any point, sometimes for incomprehensible reasons. Once such an externally created goal has been reached it can often feel worthless.

In briefly explaining these ideas I said, 'I'm wondering what the link is between the need you've described so vividly for recognition by others, which of course is needed by every human being alive, and that empty heart.' As I spoke, I briefly copied his earlier gesture and lightly struck my own chest.

For a person rarely lost for smart words, Hamish looked stunned.

'That's it. For all that I'm telling you how successful I am, I'm stressed out of my mind.' I had already noted the change in Hamish's appearance since our original social encounter. He had thickened around the waist, lost some hair, gained some lines in his face and looked pale.

Hamish had described his possessions in detail. There was the house worth many millions in a desirable part of London, the smart apartment in Edinburgh, the chateau in France and the expensive objects associated with each. He was dabbling in art but suspected he was paying over the odds for his purchases. He was buying with an eye to investment rather than because he liked the work in itself. He emphasized that there was always someone with more, someone who had a slightly better house, more valuable artwork, prettier girlfriends. When you have so many possessions you become anxious about protecting them because there could be someone planning to rob or swindle you. Your relationships sour because you become the focus of yearning attention from so many others. How do you know they like you for yourself and not for the hope that some of your fame or millions might come their way? You mix with other rich people but then you are constantly looking sideways to see whether they have slightly more or slightly less than you. Your staff become close, possibly closer than many friends, but, as he said, 'They're paid to be friends – it's not the real thing, and how do you know they won't betray you at some point?'

There was silence for a moment, then he said, 'In fact, I'm paying you. Are you another paid friend?'

'You're not paying me to be a friend. You're paying me to provide you with a safe place to think, where all the clamour in your life can be kept at bay. Yes, you're paying me for my time but that doesn't make my motives suspect. The actor who entertains you in the theatre is being paid but that doesn't make them any less interested in their craft.'

It is a truism that money does not make us happier and there are plenty of studies to show that this really is the case. After a surprisingly low level of income, happiness does not increase with more money. When you acquire a few extra millions, no one really believes you are adding millions more units of happiness to your life. Hamish referred to the myth of King Midas, saying that he believed he had 'The Midas Touch' because he had found it so easy to make money. The story tells that when

King Midas had his wish granted that everything he touched should turn to gold, he was cursed because literally everything, including his beloved daughter, did. Hamish did not know this part of the story.

'Yes,' he said slowly, 'I am that man. The week my wife left me was also the week where some jerk asked me if I had a private plane and I found myself wishing I could answer yes – and simultaneously realizing that if I did, this would be just another useless piece of junk that needed staff, money and time – and for what?'

Something about Hamish's account of his life was tugging away at me as an enigma. The extremity of his response to schoolboy taunting about his adoption and his hair colour, the fierceness of his determination to create a successful business – it seemed out of kilter with the events themselves.

At our next session I raised this question, explaining my puzzlement and saying to Hamish, 'This probably makes perfect sense to you, but it doesn't to me – join it up for me, please!'

Hamish shuffled his feet a little. 'I'm wondering whether to tell you the whole story . . . Well, yes, you're right. I held quite a lot back . . .'

At sixteen Hamish had tormented himself with the thought that his birth mother had rejected him because he was 'worthless' or that 'she was just some Glasgow slag who'd had a one-night stand'. He said he felt that there was no one he could discuss this with. At nineteen, and without telling his adoptive parents, he followed the legal process to identify his birth parents. It was easy to trace them. He found that they had both been teenagers when he was born. To his amazement he discovered that they later went to university together, married, achieved a level of professional success and had another two children: full siblings to him. They had refused to meet him, sending a stiff, formal letter through the adoption agency saying that they had remade their lives and thought it best to keep apart.

'That was the worst day of my life, getting that letter. It was simple to find out where they lived. I borrowed a car, drove to Glasgow and went to their house, a big, detached house in a nice suburb. I sat in that car, thinking, *that could have been my life.*' Hamish maintained a stony demeanour while telling me of his anger, disappointment and hurt. 'I lurked about for a long time hoping to see them, but I didn't. I felt destroyed. I was lucky not to have killed someone or myself on the motorway driving home. I went mad. I did a three-week binge.'

Hamish recovered. He turned his anger into a determination to succeed as an entrepreneur. It was important to him that his company bore his name, a visible sign of his success. His prudent risks with investment and growth paid off handsomely. He neglected his personal life. When I met him to start the coaching he was once again single after the breakdown of his second marriage and there was a succession of young, blonde, high-heeled girlfriends.

Most of us must see a purpose to our lives and one that goes beyond mere self-interest. Once we have grasped that we need this sense of purpose but do not have it, we experience what Viktor Frankl, the writer, psychiatrist and Auschwitz survivor, called 'the existential vacuum'. Frankl comments that faced with the distress of a meaningless life, we often try to fill this 'existential vacuum' with the pursuit of money or sex. Hamish and I had gone straight to that existential vacuum.

When you look for the answer to the question *What's my purpose?* you need to answer some apparently simple but probing questions. Where other people have struggled, what have you always found easy? When people praise you, what themes does this reveal? Which relationships in your life do you cherish? What personal values would you defend to the hilt? When you look at who you *are* as opposed to what you *do*, what are you most proud of? When you reflect on those moments when you are using your innate skills to achieve something that is stretching and worthwhile – what has been going on? What unachieved goals do you still have in your life? What legacy would you like to leave to the world?

These were not easy conversations. They stretched over several sessions. The language of war was still there, though it softened as the discussions went on.

Hamish's great gift was for growing companies. He was proud of another gift that he had not previously recognized – for developing people. Unlike many entrepreneurs, he had understood from the start that he needed to give away control and that to do this he had to hire people astutely, invest in their learning and offer them mentoring. He had created many jobs and had always been popular with his workforce.

Despite the loving environment created by his parents, something had still left Hamish with the suspicion that he was not loveable, and therefore it was better not to invest in an intimate relationship because that way you avoided getting hurt. Devoting himself to the acquisition of money was a way of trying to control a world that felt uncontrollable. Fleeting relationships with women almost young enough to be his daughter were a distraction from the tangles and emotional honesty needed for genuine intimacy, but they had also wrecked his marriages.

'Yeah, wealth attracts gold-diggers all right, and some of them are very clever in making you think that it's you they love, not your power, money and status.'

At our penultimate session we returned again to the themes that had dominated our conversations. I asked Hamish to say in a few sentences how he would like his life to be in future. He replied calmly, with no military language or challenge to me.

'I want to simplify my life. I want a healthy relationship with a woman. I want kids. I want to do something that matters.'

Clients do not make immediate dramatic changes as a result of coaching. The change may take months or years to develop and consolidate. Hamish did not impulsively give away his millions nor fall instantly in love with a woman of his own age. He did not retrain as a teacher nor volunteer to do humble work in an impoverished country. There was no sentimental reunion with his birth parents or his siblings. He did sell some of his assets and there were fewer trophy girlfriends. But once an entrepreneur, always an entrepreneur. He set up an enterprise that had a charitable arm and a trading arm. It included an ingenious mentoring scheme. Grants were given, shrewd strings attached, to aspiring young entrepreneurs with unpromising personal histories, many of which involved exclusion from school, being in care or sometimes in prison. The charitable arm was doing well and the trading arm was making money. As he said to me in an email a little later, 'King Midas found his heart.'

Often, the client's most carefully buried fear is that they cannot change and that they are the victim of their experience, of their genetic heritage, their childhood or of some character flaw. By refusing to behave as the rest of the world does towards them – whether this is rejection and disapproval or exploitation and sycophancy – a coach conveys that change is possible. Hamish took the risk of exposing what he believed was his worst possible self to me. He probably exaggerated the supposed wickedness of this self. In the same way he conducted his other relationships, it was about nerve, simultaneously playful and deadly serious. The unspoken test was, 'Do you like me? Am I likeable? Can you stand it even when I describe my acquisitiveness and the shallowness of my relationships? Are you shocked?'

Working with Hamish could have been taxing for me. At the time, my husband's level of disability was rising rapidly. Although he continued working right up until the day before his death, his physical helplessness had been accelerated by an accident in which, already made clumsy by muscular weakness, he had overturned his wheelchair and broken his shoulder.

This disastrous event meant he could not feed himself nor attend to any of his bodily functions. The cost of making his life easier was astonishingly high, steadily eroding our life savings. Like Hamish, we had more than one home, but unlike him, there was an enormous mortgage on the second home, a place Alan loved as it was a house skilfully designed for someone in a wheelchair. To help pay for it all, I felt I had to work flat out with little time for leisure, economizing fiercely on discretionary expenditure. Anxiety about money was my perpetual companion. At one level it might have been hard to listen to Hamish talking about being oppressed by his many millions. Bitterness and envy might have been tempting: what a welcome problem it would apparently have been to have had too much money. These thoughts did fleetingly cross my mind. Just a fraction of one of those millions would have solved a lot of our problems.

At the same time, Hamish's marital difficulties were a reminder of how hard marriage can be. Nature did not equip me to be a carer, yet that was what I was now required to be, taking my place in the rota along with the people we paid and with other members of the family. I am not proud of the disappointment and irrational sense of betrayal I felt at the hard work it took to help Alan with tasks that are so easy for an able-bodied person, such as putting on socks or turning over in bed. I mourned the loss of the easy-going companionship that had been the hallmark of our marriage. Where previously it had been a partnership of equals, now he was dependent on me. When I blithely married my husband in my early twenties I had no clue that decades later I would be wiping his bottom. There were the tensions, there was physical exhaustion, yet the connection between us was unbreakable. Despite the toll it took on us all to look after him, I knew that the marriage and all the other close relationships would endure.

All of this was at its height when I was working with Hamish. The obviousness of the contrast somehow helped me. I had no doubt that Hamish was at a crisis point in his life and that, despite his jokes, his unhappiness was overwhelming enough to engage in a process – coaching – that privately he probably continued to believe was all a bit of a con. I was also at a crisis point, but mine was different. When he teasingly but nonetheless seriously invited me to envy him, or to admire his lifestyle or his sexual prowess, or to compete with him about which of us was the more successful in our worlds, my own problems made it easy to stay separate. I ended every session feeling thankful that my husband, family and friends could put up with me and knowing that in working with him to identify his life purpose, I was fulfilling my own.

When Hamish had said, 'I want to simplify my life,' I remember having given him a wry smile. I'd replied, 'Yes, that's exactly what I want too, so that's one thing we have in common.'

Some years later we met in a London hotel bar for a catch-up drink. He looked slim, fit and relaxed. He said he was on his way to dinner with a colleague, a person with whom, as he shyly admitted, he had developed 'a wonderful relationship'. She sounded like a good choice.

'So, um, did you simplify your life?' he asked, with the air of someone hastily remembering his manners. He knew that my husband had died since we had worked together.

'Well remembered. Yes, I have. I now just work part-time and I choose my clients carefully. I got on with the horrible task of bereavement, I sold the second home – it was at a loss, but it was a relief. I sorted out the debts. And thank you,' I slid a glance at him as I said this, 'you won't know it, but you helped with all of that.'

Hamish looked a little bemused. But he was smiling, gathering his things together to rush off for his date, and I don't think he heard.

New Life

When you ask coaches what kinds of client they most relish, they will invariably tell you that they look for people who are eager learners, motivated, self-aware, clear about what they want and ready to be challenged as well as supported.

Yet at one point in my coaching career, when I was still relatively new to coaching, it felt that few of my clients met these criteria. It seemed that the sponsors in organizations, those senior people who spotted a need for coaching and acted as brokers, were sending me people who were the exact opposite of this perfect client. These were the problem children, often on a last chance to cling to their jobs, everyone around them offended, annoyed, embarrassed, irritated, avoiding them wherever possible.

The clients themselves were frequently sullen, sorry for themselves and full of long-winded counter-accusations about how they had been bullied, sidelined and misunderstood. They were victims in their own eyes. They would maintain this was true even when one of the charges against them was that they had bullied and victimized others. I was becoming the go-to coach for the Billy-No-Mates, the failures, the potential outcasts. Often in such circumstances the organization has already given up on them. Coaching can be an empty gesture before the final execution: 'See, we really tried, we found them a great coach, but it was hopeless.' This is disheartening work for the coach. Though few of us admit it, we want that little ego stroke, we want to be associated with success, to say that we work with the starry people so that a little of their sparkle falls on us, to feel that we have made a difference, otherwise why are we doing this work at all? To have a client who fails means that failure attaches to the coach, however unfairly. It was our job to save them from themselves and we didn't do it.

Madison seemed to be one such client. She was forty-five and had been brought from Chicago as a senior economist to run a team in her firm's London office. It had taken less than six months for her boss to decide that she either changed her behaviour or she was out.

'I can't fault her work ethic,' he said, 'she's obsessive, but that's part of the problem. She hides in her office, goes missing without explanation, is silent in meetings, gets even more silent if you challenge her. Or else she mumbles that she's the expert and this is why we hired her in the first place so why don't we just trust her to get on with the job?'

It was August, one of those hot, late-summer days in London that feels airless and sleepy. Madison was sitting in the coaching room based in my then home, a tall, thin house built by a canny speculator in 1827. Against all odds the house had survived neglect, overcrowding, soot, slum landlords, two wars and the drying out of its London clay foundations. This last had left it with a number of lopsided floors and doorways that were not quite rectangular. It had been rescued in the 1970s when at last London had soot-free air and people like me saw the beauty and grace of its many Georgian terraces, despite their dilapidated appearance.

I loved this house with its sunlit rooms and long, admittedly rather badly fitting sash windows. It had been a comfortable place to bring up a family. I had turned what had been humble outbuildings into a purpose-designed coaching space. This jutted from the lower ground floor with simple French doors opening into a shady little garden paved with York stone. The oversized pots of fruit trees and shrubs added what I thought of proudly as a quirky touch of style.

My first meeting with Madison had not gone well. Her severe black jacket remained tightly buttoned, she hugged her boxy leather briefcase. She sat stiffly, giving minimal answers to my questions. She expressed surprise that I worked from home and it seemed to me that she glanced disdainfully at my pretty garden. It was not a promising beginning.

The starting issue for clients like Madison is to acknowledge that there is a problem and that at least part of it has its roots in their own behaviour. If the client can't acknowledge that there's a problem then this becomes the problem. With Madison's reluctant consent, I interviewed a dozen of her colleagues and wrote up my findings. The consensus was that, while she was clearly a brilliant thinker, Madison was isolated. They found her aloof, baffling and disengaged.

Now it was our second meeting and I had just given her my report to read. I had opened the French doors but it still felt sultry in what was usually a cool room. Even the garden birds seemed silenced by the heat and humidity.

Madison's mouth was a hard, thin line. Despite the high temperature, she had not taken off or unbuttoned her jacket. She was gripping the heavy briefcase and I noticed its sharp corners and substantial metal locks. I briefly contemplated asking her to put it on the floor and then thought, mmm, maybe not.

'This feedback stuff is crazy,' she said. Her words were clipped. I couldn't read her expression. 'I'm a statistician, and I promise that you'd never get a PhD with this stuff.' She took my report by one corner and held it up. 'What does it mean, "*Some* people said..." or "*A few* people thought..." How many is some, how many is a few?'

'It's qualitative not quantitative data. It's impressionistic. You remember that I explained the methodology when we had our first session?'

Madison's face was blank. 'I don't know what to make of it. Do they hate me?'

'Of course not, but I think they're puzzled. And let's not lose sight of the fact that they clearly respect your professional expertise.'

'For whatever that's worth.' She shrugged with a slight curl of the lip, suggesting that the respect was not mutual.

I heard light footsteps on the stairs leading down to the coaching room. There was a tap on the door. It was Angie, my PA.

'Jenny, I'm really sorry to interrupt but you're needed upstairs.'

This was an unheard-of event. I immediately felt anxious: it would have to be an emergency of some sort. I registered Madison's frown. I imagined her wondering what kind of a coach was this who had such a homespun office, would never be capable of getting a PhD with her sloppy research and allowed staff to intrude?

Anxiety had in fact been my constant companion over the previous three months. Feelings of loss had been triggered by the death of a dear friend of my own age, B, who had stubbornly refused to acknowledge that chemotherapy and radiotherapy were the only solutions for her rare and aggressive cancer. Instead, in her vulnerability, she had fallen prey to people peddling a bogus cancer cure. Her oncologist had listened carefully but had told her there was no evidence that drinking several litres of blended raw vegetables a day could cure cancer and that such a diet could potentially make her general health worse. Her reply was that he had been bamboozled by the evil pharmaceutical companies. I had implored B to listen to him. Instead she had paid money she could ill afford to travel to a 'clinic' in another country for coffee enemas, reflexology, reiki, crystal therapy and yet more of the horrible juices. I was haunted by the certainty that if only I had been able to do a better job of persuasion, her life would have been prolonged. She had deteriorated rapidly. In her final month she had withdrawn completely to the care of a brother and his wife. They had created an exclusion zone around her, doubtless at her instruction. I had not been able to say goodbye. There had been a small private funeral and I had not been invited.

Along with this intense and unresolved sorrow had been the vague understanding that my days of active parenting were over. My elder son had left home and the younger son was at university. The big old house felt empty, just me and a husband whose health was visibly worsening. He needed yet another hip replacement. A house with ninety stairs was maybe going to prove impossible for someone who had such difficulty walking, but I was doing my best to avoid thinking about it. I felt profoundly unhappy at the prospect of leaving it.

Upstairs, Angie had disappeared into her own office. This was the former playroom in the house, a room I had crammed with filing cabinets, untidy piles of books and boxes of papers.

I was astonished to see my younger son, Owen, home unexpectedly, looking a little pink but holding my gaze.

'I'm sorry to interrupt, Mum, but I've got to get a train in just under an hour. I wanted to tell you straight away. You probably won't like what I've got to say, but Maria and I are having a baby. It isn't what we planned but don't tell me we have to get an abortion. We've seen it on a scan and there's no way we're going to kill it.'

I had the impression this speech had been rehearsed many times. He hurried on.

'We both really want to be parents. We're going to drop out of university. We've made up our minds. We know what people will say, we don't care, we've discussed it so don't try to talk us out of it. I'll get some kind of a job. We'll make it work somehow.'

What went through my mind? They're only nineteen. They're too young to be parents. It's a shotgun relationship and it won't last. They could finish their courses with the right childcare. I know what everyone will say, that they're ruining their lives. My dad will be furious, he'll think it's shameful, he'll think they should get married and I know that won't even occur to them. How will they get proper jobs without degrees? They can't possibly know what they're up against. We'll have to help them financially.

Yet in this moment my true feeling was one of pure joy. I was going to be a grandmother! I recognized immediately that changing the minds of these very young prospective parents was impossible. I recognized their pluck in facing up to their responsibilities. I recognized their refusal to be victims or to take the easy way out. I had a flashback to this son as a four-year-old successfully pestering me to buy him a 'proper boy doll' and a doll's pram, remembering too that the girls in the street had mocked him mercilessly: dolls and prams were for girls, silly! That doll had been named 'Frank'. For a wild moment I imagined a boy grandchild called Frank.

I enveloped my son in a big hug. 'Your dad and I will do whatever is needed to support all three of you,' I said. 'I'll call you and we'll talk properly later.'

Angie reappeared, giving me a questioning look. I smiled and did not explain. 'Make another pot of tea, Ange, put it on our best tray and bring it downstairs with that pretty china and the matching milk jug.'

I bounced back down the stairs.

Madison looked up warily. It was impossible to hold back my elation. I was aware that I was babbling.

'I'm going to be a granny! They're only nineteen, they're too young and so naive and they say they'll drop out of university, but it feels right! Please help me celebrate. Angie is bringing us some more tea.'

Madison stared at me glassily for a moment. Then a small smile appeared. Speaking so quietly I could hardly hear her, she blurted out, 'That's wonderful. Congratulations! I have a little grandchild, just the one. I don't see her. I'm estranged from my daughter, she's very young too, and she's a single parent and my only family. She sided with my ex-husband when we split up. It's one of the reasons I agreed to come to the UK, to get away and make a fresh start, a new life.'

How was it that everything changed in that moment? But it did.

The big briefcase was placed carefully on the floor. She undid her jacket. With a flourish, I poured tea into the special cups.

I said, 'I think somehow we've taken a wrong turning in this coaching. Let's start again. Let's imagine that this is our first session. Tell me what you need from me.'

Slowly, Madison began to speak.

'I don't seem to be able to relate to people here. I can't hear your accents properly, often I've got no idea what people are saying and sometimes they seem to be glowering at me and don't get me either.'

'What don't they get?'

'Who I am!'

'What might you do to help them get who you are?'

Madison shook her head. She looked helpless and vulnerable, a hunched figure in a jacket that now appeared too big for her.

'I've lost heart. I really don't know.'

Psychometric questionnaires are a valuable shortcut to self-awareness. Without self-awareness we struggle to understand why particular patterns and problems repeat themselves in our lives and to accept that the common factor is us, not other people. When I debriefed Madison's results on one questionnaire, a Jungian approach to personality, they showed how strong her preference for introversion was. Here, introversion does not mean the neurotic handicap of a self-absorbed, unconfident person, but a need to get energy from reflection and privacy. Too much talking, too many people, too much interaction is simply exhausting. But those of us with a preference for introversion need to learn how to manage it, including how to get good enough at its psychological opposite, extraversion. We also need to understand that being introverted can easily be mistaken for being cool, critical, arrogant or shy. Other people are not mind readers. In the absence of explanation, they will construe their own fantasies about us. In Madison's case, her natural preference for private thinking was combining disastrously with her failure to make any kind of breakthrough in understanding British society or the particular culture of her London office.

'People have said that you disappear from the office from time to time,' I said. 'What's going on there?'

What was going on was that Madison had a serious gynaecological problem which involved sudden cramps, a lot of pain and frightening haemorrhages.

'A horrific thing happened in my first week here,' she said. 'The back of my skirt was soaked in blood and I couldn't stem it. I had to tie my coat around my waist and get myself home somehow, then later I had to throw all those clothes away. I was afraid to get a taxi in case I leaked on to the seat. It was so embarrassing.' A number of times since then, feeling the first indications that another such event was about to happen, she had left the office suddenly and rushed home.

Fearful of Britain's public healthcare system and with no experience of how to navigate it, she had not yet registered with a GP and was still depending on a clinician in Chicago with whom she had remained in contact. She had told no one in her firm about this problem and seemed unaware that unexplained sudden absences would cause speculation and gossip.

Madison was lonely. Her marriage had felt empty for many years and had ended in bitterness after she had a brief affair with a colleague. The divorce was acrimonious and the settlement left her feeling disadvantaged. Their daughter – hurt, frightened and angry – had blamed her for the break-up, refused to meet and had banned all contact with her child.

I noticed that Madison spoke in true introverted style, in brief, carefully thought-through sentences quietly delivered. It would be easy to miss the intensity and sometimes cryptic content of their meaning. Saying things once is often not enough, especially if the words have been delivered at low volume by someone whose habit in meetings is to let other people do most of the talking and then to give up too easily when others fail to let you into the conversation. Then there was her 'resting face', the unguarded look we all have when we believe we are unobserved. In Madison's case it was notably inscrutable or possibly a little frowny.

In the work we subsequently did together, Madison first had to learn to make her thinking and motivation visible through words and facial expression. She had to learn how to be an enthusiastic advocate for the advantages of introversion: an ability to listen attentively, to create relationships of depth, to offer measured comment. She did this. She successfully championed the introduction of 'quiet rooms' for small meetings and private thinking as well as flexible working for those who could work better from home on at least one day a week. She learnt to smile more and frown less. She told her boss about her medical condition and met immediate sympathy and concern.

'Since I've come out as an introvert,' Madison said, smiling, 'I've discovered that there are a lot of us in the company.' She reported that it had become common for people to say, 'Nothing personal – but I need some I-Time,' her own phrase for explaining that introverts need uninterrupted space to recharge their energies.

Madison and I discussed the whole question of Anglo-American language. When I first started working with her she was socially isolated and seemed to have made no modifications to her American vocabulary. We agreed that there was a hierarchy of needs here. First, she needed to learn British versions of corporate lingo in order to make herself understood – and to understand. Then she had to learn which words seemed to be the same but had different meanings in each country, for instance 'school' for 'university'. Finally, she had to know which words would mark her as an outsider and to decide whether or not this mattered enough to change them.

Madison made her own well-calibrated choices on all of this. When in London she started saying that people were *clever* rather than *smart*. She became comfortable with expressing temperature in centigrade. She cooked with grams, not cups. She could bandy London bus routes, *routes* pronounced the British way of course, with colleagues.

She made some close British friends. She was promoted at work and with their help negotiated a visa with 'indefinite leave to remain' in the UK. She had successful surgery at the expense of the British taxpayer, one of whose number she had become. Cautiously, she renewed contact with her daughter and the fractured relationship was to some extent pasted back together.

The writer William Bridges has written eloquently in his book *Transitions* about the differences between the formal start of a new phase in life and our actual adjustment to it. He points out that even where we have freely chosen a new direction, there is still a sense of loss, so the psychological adjustment, that is, our acknowledgement that something really has ended, happens much later than the formal ending. Where we have not chosen the change and it has been imposed, the adjustment takes longer still. We get dismayed, muddled about what is really over and at the same time uncertain about what has really begun. He calls this middle phase of confusion and discomfort 'The Neutral Zone'. I believe a Neutral Zone is healthy and necessary, often a time of creativity and openness to learning. It seemed that this was what Madison was experiencing.

On that August day more than two decades ago there was a serendipitous triangle, a coming together of new life. Madison saw that her time in Chicago was over. It was the start of accepting that her personal style needed adjustment because it was not helping her adapt to a new country and a new life. She acknowledged that she urgently needed surgical treatment and that there was no point in empty stoicism. For my part, I at last grasped that my dear friend B had the right to choose the manner of her death even if it had excluded me and that this did not reflect on the quality of our long friendship. I suddenly remembered that the last time I had seen her, she had said, enigmatically, 'We die in the middle of a sentence.' I now understood what she meant, that it was a goodbye message for me. I realized that a beloved house would soon have to be sold, that bitterness about this loss was pointless and that I would be moving into a different phase of my own life as a newly enrolled member of the older generation. My business was growing and it needed proper offices. My son made the thrilling pregnancy public; it could no longer be a secret. He was going to be a father.

Sponsors still sent me challenging cases, but I no longer received them with the same negative feelings that these initially unenthusiastic clients were expressing with me. Instead I began to realize that it was often time for them to move on. Their misery and hostility were as much about knowing they were in the wrong jobs as it was about anger with their employers. I developed expertise and confidence in career coaching, thanks to this unsought experience. When they looked back, most of these clients saw their problems as the kick-start they had needed and virtually all of them eventually made the transition to more satisfying lives. Coaching itself has moved on since that time: it is no longer seen as a secret process for people who are failing. Instead it has become a highly sought reward for promotion.

Recently I was reminiscing about that August day with my son.

Although we have discussed that turning point many times, he was still curious. 'What was literally your first thought when I told you?'

It was easy to reply as I remember it so vividly. Later I did the maths and realized, thanks to various indiscreet hints from the young parents (whose little son, by the way, was not named Frank, who are still together and who have another child, both now young adults), that the day of this baby's conception was also the day of B's death.

'My thought was, when one life ends, a new life begins.'

Being Real

Impostor

When coaches talk about having a 'supervisor' they don't mean
that this person is their boss. They mean a fellow coach, often
someone more experienced, with whom they have an arrange-
ment to discuss in confidence the knottier aspects of their work.
It's an imprecise process. As a supervisor you never observe the
coach at work and have no formal control of any kind over them.
If they wished, they could spin you a series of silkily told yarns
and it could take you a while to discover that it was all hooey.

As it turned out, hooey was exactly the issue with Alicia.

Alicia had been a coach for twelve years and in that time had
built a thriving practice concentrating largely on clients in the
financial services sector. Coaching is unlike some other professions such as accountancy or medicine in that it is an option. If
everything is going perfectly in your life you do not need a coach,
and coaching clients do not normally need or want a continuing
relationship with the practitioner so coaches must have a con-
tinuous pipeline of new clients if they are to make a living. Alicia
had managed this triumphantly. She told me she was always busy,
so busy that she sometimes had to say no to potential clients.

Yet Alicia confessed she was haunted by the feeling that she
was an impostor.

'Some mornings I wake up convinced that today is the day
someone will tap me on the shoulder and say, "You do know you
are a sham, don't you?" Then all my work will disappear and my
clients will tell each other that I fooled them for a bit but they
always knew I was rubbish.'

The uneasy feeling that her success was somehow a mistake
had been exacerbated by a recent piece of work with a challenging

finance director client. This man was at the centre of an unpleasant media attack on his competence. The HR director in his organization had suggested coaching as one way of supporting someone so uncomfortably in the public eye. Part of the issue for this client was that he displayed a stubborn independence, a refusal to take advice or accept other points of view and a tendency to blame colleagues for his difficulties. Alicia told me that she had felt herself shrink at the beginning of their first session.

The client had turned to her beadily and demanded, 'Tell me, what's the evidence that coaching works? What are your qualifications for doing this work, exactly? What, if anything, do you know about finance?'

In the same supervision session, Alicia sought my help in dealing with anxiety about giving presentations. Her eyes clouded as she told me that she was beginning to recognize a pattern. At first she felt euphoric to have been asked to contribute, for instance to a high-profile conference where she would talk about the value of coaching. It was an honour and also a marketing opportunity as so many potential clients would usually be present. This elation was short-lived as it was always closely followed by intense anxiety.

She said, 'I torment myself with feeling that I have nothing new to say, that they will be bored, that they will see through me, so I sleep badly, have dreams about drying up and people scoffing at me. I procrastinate and then overprepare. It can take me two days to get my slides ready, even when I'm just adapting them from other presentations which seem to have gone well. On my way to the last event I caught myself wishing that I could literally break a leg as an excuse not to be there. I got a lot of acclaim from that event. Again, I felt euphoria for a short while but then all the other feelings came back. I was certain they'd only applauded to be nice to me, or because, as they told me, I'm a "glamorous woman", and I was certain that all the other speakers would get better feedback.'

'And what feedback did you actually get?'

Alicia squirmed a little. 'I have to admit it was all positive.'

Despite the obvious stress it caused, Alicia could not resist the opportunity to seek more occasions where she would repeat the same cycle. In her coaching work, she told me that she often seemed to attract challenging clients and found it virtually impossible to turn them away.

Alicia's feelings are common and well-enough recognized to have a name: Impostor Syndrome. This is so widespread that there is every reason to suppose that the human species specializes in deception, taking on roles a lot of the time that, like actors who have only half learnt a part, we feel we cannot properly play.

The typical sufferer from Impostor Syndrome inflates all of this to a level where it is interfering with their life. Typically, they are a gifted overachiever who cannot accept their own talent. The self-labelled 'impostor' secretly believes that their success is a mistake, that other people are invariably smarter and that their own achievements are a fluke. They overwork, they find it difficult to delegate, they define their lives by the number of hours they spend at the office, they burn out, they suffer from insomnia, they worry about whether they are next on the redundancy list.

It is worth pointing out to these self-styled impostors that they are nothing like the real thing: people whose entire lives are clotted with lies and grotesque deception. Examples include Bernard Madoff, who swindled thousands of people out of their life savings, Frank Abagnale, who successfully impersonated pilots, doctors and professors, or Laurens van der Post, who managed to convince many influential people, including British royalty, that he was an expert on the Bushmen of the Kalahari when it seems unlikely that this was wholly true.

A few weeks after our session I had an email from Alicia. The tone was quiet desperation. The challenging finance director client had complained about her to the HR gatekeeper and had refused to continue with the coaching, lightly sneering at the process as 'just a nice chat with a charming person but it seems to be therapy for well people, and I can do without that. I haven't got time to waste on all that navel-gazing nonsense. It's smoke and mirrors. It's about as much use as tarot cards or astrology.'

Alicia was in despair. It seemed that her worst fear had come true: a client had called her a fake and had dismissively described her as 'charming'. It's possible that Alicia was offended or surprised by my enthusiastic response to this apparently terrible event, as despite sincerely expressing sympathy for the reality of her feelings, I refused to see it as a tragedy. Professional work of any kind cannot consistently be delivered at the level of genius, something most self-styled impostors secretly believe should be possible. Most of us do mediocre or good-enough work most of the time with, maybe, occasional spikes of brilliance if we are lucky.

Some failure is inevitable and an obvious failure is to be embraced, not dreaded. Something imperfect or disappointing has occurred, but is it really a disaster? What is to be learnt from it? How will you recover? How will it look in a year's time? How does this single failure fit with the many successes? What does it say about the other party in the 'failure' that this event occurred?

It was time to look more generally at the impostor belief. I asked her to treat it as if it were a person and to tell me its history.

Alicia had a younger brother and had always felt at a disadvantage in relation to him, saying that her parents had early on categorized Richard as 'the clever one' and her as 'the charming one'. The family was affluent, yet it was made clear to the children that their education was expensive and that hard work was expected in return. Both went to highly academic schools and did equally well. Yet Richard's achievements seemed to be constantly lauded while she felt patronized about her own. 'I felt that whatever I did the reaction would be, "Jolly good – for Alicia".' Often she felt a sense of disapproval and disappointment, and she said that her parents would make critical remarks about her children, for instance that their table manners were not perfect, 'but what can you expect when you work full-time, it's not as if you can be there to correct them, is it?'

Richard had thrived for a while but in his late thirties his drug and alcohol problems began to increase. His marriage broke down. At the time I was working with Alicia he had returned for the second time to his parents' home. Periods of treatment in costly private facilities were interspersed with sporadic efforts to resume his career.

'My parents are totally in denial about him,' Alicia said. 'He's still their golden boy and he's ruining their retirement with his tiresome behaviour.'

It was a new thought to Alicia that her brother may well also have been experiencing Impostor Syndrome. Here the story may be of a child who is over-praised, who secretly suspects that the praise is unjustified and becomes paralysed by the need to keep up appearances. In these cases the sufferer dreads becoming successful and then being unable to perform at the level they believe is needed.

Alicia paused at one point in her recital. 'I need to tell you something awful, something that I've never told anyone,' she said.

'Okay – I think I'm unshockable, so go ahead.'

As a first-year undergraduate, Alicia had a humble vacation job as a clerk with an examinations board, the same one that her school had used. Haunted by impostor feelings even then and sure that her outstanding exam results must have been a mistake, Alicia had found an excuse to get into their archives. She rooted out her own papers and discovered that for one History paper, in theory her strongest subject and the result she believed had earnt her the place at Oxford, she had only received 69 per cent.

'I was so ashamed,' she said, 'I smuggled that script into my bag, took it home and tore it up. So you see,' she went on, avoiding my eyes, 'it really was a mistake. I never should have got that high grade and probably the only reason I got into Oxford was because, just as my parents always told me, I was *charming*. I was probably seductive in the interview. That professor just fell for a pretty girl. And that's exactly what that client said – I was *charming* – I hate that word. And now I'm admitting to you that I'm a petty thief as well!'

One of my clients once accused me, and I don't think he meant it as a compliment, of being a *lady-jackdaw-person-collector* because according to him I often seemed to know someone who knew someone who knew someone who might be helpful. In this case I had a contact whose special obsession is the history of public examinations in the UK. This person can drone on until listeners beg him to stop on topics such as *rubrics, grade boundaries, criterion referencing, scaling, moderating, distractors in multiple-choice questions, demographic changes, bell curves* and *random distributions* – and on and infinitely on. It was a mercifully swift matter to establish from him that at the time when Alicia took A-level History, the raw score on her script would have been merely the starting point and that marks would have been subjected to various human and statistical manipulations. She had earnt her top grade, it was not a mistake.

Alicia made the appropriate phone call to my contact and reported its result with a shamefaced smile.

'And the word *charming*,' I said, 'since when was that the antonym of *clever*? Might it be possible and actually desirable to be clever *and* charming?'

At about this time I read in my newspaper that Alicia's would-have-been finance director client had 'stepped down'. His departure was sweetened by a generous financial package and, who knows, maybe he had the offer of another coach to help him get over the shock of losing his job.

Alicia had described how her negative beliefs might have been created and I asked her to tell me how she saw them in her mind. 'If you had to visualize them, what form would they take?'

'They would be like large sinister insects,' she replied instantly. 'But one or two of them we seem to have swatted down.'

'Can we give them names?'

Alicia knew this game as it is one that is taught to many coaches during their training. The idea is that by turning your negative beliefs into ridiculous beings with silly names, you limit their ability to destroy your confidence.

'Yes,' she said, 'there'd be Willie Wasp. A wasp because he buzzes around saying, "You have to take this piece of work because it could be the last you'll ever get and that's because any minute now they will see through you!" Then there's Hard Hattie the Hornet. She says, "Pride comes before a fall and you're nothing like as good as you say you are. If only people knew!" And then there's Subtle Simon the Smirking Spider. His role is to say, "People are laughing at you, but you don't know how ridiculous you are!"'

There is a difference between beliefs that are genuinely helpful and beliefs that are destructive. Alicia and I discussed these distinctions. It is not helpful to believe you are an impostor if it leads, as it usually does, to procrastination, perfectionism and to doing entirely unnecessary work. But at the same time, most of us when in the grip of Impostor Syndrome cling to the idea that the procrastination, perfectionism and overwork are exactly what has led to whatever success we have experienced. The question for discussion is to what extent this is correct and to what extent it is a delusion. It's always possible that you might do better work and achieve more if you worked less.

The most powerful of Alicia's imaginary insect tormentors was Willie Wasp. His annoying buzzing and potential to sting typically sprang to life when she was invited to talk to a group of other coaches. 'Surely they will see that I know nothing more than they do?' she asked. One of these invitations had now come her way, so it would be a test of how successfully the pestilential activity of Willie Wasp could be controlled.

*

At about the same time that Alicia and I were discussing this topic, a newspaper did a feature about executive coaching. It included profiles of several coaches, one of them Alicia. She was described as 'an outstandingly successful coach'. The article mentioned how much income she made in a typical year and included a handsome photograph. Instead of feeling pleased and flattered by this free publicity, Alicia called me in angry tears.

'My father has just been on the phone. He and my brother have read that piece and he told me they'd roared with laughter at it. He said it was ridiculous that I earnt so much money from a "trivial" thing like coaching which isn't even a proper profession and probably depends on my ability to "schmooze" people. He said he didn't know what I thought I was doing posing for a "Page 3 picture".'

One of the tasks of any coach is to help clients look squarely at habitual patterns of dysfunctional communication. This will usually establish that however appalling the behaviour of the other person, you will more often than not have some responsibility for how the relationship has developed. It will also involve acknowledging that you can never know other people's motivation and that there are myriad possibilities to explain their behaviour. It's a choice: do you continue as it has always been or do you decide to change? If the latter, you will have to accept that you cannot change others, you can only change yourself.

Alicia and I discussed how she should deal with her parents and brother at the forthcoming Sunday lunch that she had been dreading.

'If you were at your calmest and most resilient, what would you like to say to them?'

Alicia had no doubt what this would be. It would not be an 'and another thing' diatribe about her upbringing. She would not be angry, tearful or sorrowful. She would say that she now had a choice about accepting or disagreeing with their view of her and could live freely with the outcome. She would assume they were joking and not serious in their response to the article. She would assume their comments about her profession were a clumsy attempt at humour. Instead of falling into the old habit of defensive arguing, she would ask them to say more about their views. She would ask them what they knew about coaching. Then she would enquire into whether they would like to hear more about her work. And if they showed no interest, she would end it there.

I suggested a further tweak on these excellent ideas: the martial arts tactic of unexpectedly stepping back and letting your opponent fall over with his own momentum. In this case it would mean light-hearted agreement with her father and brother. I suggested she should agree for instance that coaching is an unregulated profession which contains many charlatans. To agree that it is often impossible to say how effective your work has been. To agree that coaching is just two people in a room talking. To agree that some coaches do charge high fees – because the work needs psychological competence, business nous, the confidence to work with very senior people, ability to tolerate ambiguity, high levels of self-management plus comprehensive knowledge of the organization world.

Alicia prepared for her conference presentation. She had decided to experiment with doing the minimum of preparation. It was a conference that I had already decided to attend. There were several hundred coaches of many nationalities and ages, and in the general melee of registration I noticed a slim, white-haired man leaning on a cane. Increasingly, I appear to be among the oldest participants at these events and I found it encouraging to see someone within shouting distance of my own generation: we coaches can go on happily into old age, I thought.

Alicia was gracefully introduced by a senior figure in the coaching world. She stood up, beaming, looking every inch the commanding figure she was.

'Ladies and gentlemen, fellow coaches. I'm going to talk to you today about Impostor Syndrome, something a vast number of our clients experience and think is a shameful secret. But as we know, the way to deal with a shameful secret is to expose it because that takes away its power. I am one of the world's leading experts on Impostor Syndrome because I have suffered from it myself for years, and this is one subject on which I know for certain that I am not a fake!'

Laughter rippled around the room.

'And,' she said, whipping out and waving a handful of giddily-coloured, strange puppet-like objects on sticks, 'I want to introduce you to my friends Willie Wasp, Hard Hattie the Hornet and Subtle Simon the Smirking Spider.' Later I was to discover that these objects had been skilfully manufactured from papier mâché by Alicia's ten-year-old daughter. This, according to Alicia, kept her promise to me about minimal preparation because it was her daughter who did all the work.

After the presentation was over, Alicia found me. She was gently tugging along a smiling, slightly built, white-haired gentleman leaning on a cane, whom I could now see was rather frail.

'Jenny,' she said, turning tenderly to her companion, 'I really want you to meet my dad.'

Sleuths

This assignment was a failure. Looking back, I am astonished that I was unable to piece together the picture that later became so clear.

My respect and liking for Harry had grown. He had become an impressive leader without losing his unique blend of humour and fierce concentration on business success. Over the time that I had been his coach, I had also got to know and like many of his team, including Sara, who had started as his PA and who now ran a small team herself, a reflection of the rapid way the business had expanded. She and I bumped into each other occasionally at a local Pilates studio where we exchanged self-pitying complaints about how mercilessly the teachers worked us.

Harry needed to make a new senior appointment and there were some strong candidates already on the staff. My brief was loose. What Harry wanted was a light-touch assessment to be done any way I liked as long as it was seen to be fair. He told me that he was perfectly capable of making up his own mind.

'But I want the benefit of any insights you have into these characters,' he said. 'I'm too close to them and I daresay my ideas about them have got too fixed. I'd like to hear a bit more about what makes them tick. Come back to me with your observations plus questions that I might ask when we get to the actual selection stage.'

In this preparatory discussion Harry confessed that he was leaning more towards Jake, the newest to the company of the three candidates. 'He's got flair, he's got energy. He's very personable but he also knows how to press people to get what we want.' At the same time, Harry acknowledged that the other two contenders had earnt their right to promotion with a history of delivering excellent results and of developing loyal teams.

Keeping it simple seemed like the best approach. I told Harry I would ask each of the trio to send me their CV, and would spend two hours getting them to talk me through their early lives and then their careers, looking for themes that would highlight their needs, skills and motivation. In a subsequent session I would offer a full personal debrief on a number of psychometric questionnaires. This would include a discussion about how far they agreed with any of the data that came out of the analysis and where they saw their strengths and weaknesses in relation to the new job. Then I proposed shadowing each of them for half a day at work. After that I would have an unhurried conversation with Harry about what I had seen, adding some suggestions about topics that he and colleagues might want to explore during the interviews; I would play no part in the interviews themselves.

The three people were duly informed. If they made any protests about having to go through this process, I never heard them. The purpose of the exercise was described openly and it was pitched to them as a development experience, at least in part, and there would have been nothing unfamiliar about it to people who had already experienced assessment centres, commonly used in many organizations for recruitment and promotion.

I had already learnt through Sara that Jake, the relative newcomer, was 'rather dashing' and had also made a few enemies through his eagerness to introduce change.

At our first session, Jake appeared at my apartment with flowers. Not a limp bunch of dyed carnations hastily snatched from one of those buckets at a supermarket, but a proper hand-tied bouquet in a stylish box carried on soft silvery strings. I have sometimes been sent flowers by clients after a coaching programme has finished, but no one had ever previously arrived with flowers at its outset.

'I've been a bit of a sleuth,' he said, smiling cheerfully. 'I've googled you and I've been reading about you. And I guessed from your website that you might be the kind of lady who has good taste. I wanted to start off on the right foot by impressing you. I'm sure you'll see right through this as a bit pathetic, of course. And Sara told me your husband had died not that long ago – I was sorry to hear that – so I guessed maybe you might be in need of a man to bring you flowers!'

All this was unsettling. Flowers are sent with condolences, given to cheer up an invalid, as a gift for a host, as a thank you or as a symbol of courtship. They seemed to have no place in a first exchange between a coach and a client. I thanked Jake politely and set them aside to put into a vase later.

It is rare for a client to express much interest in the coach. They may ask a few perfunctory questions to seem polite, but by and large they are incurious about us. They want us to be wise, omniscient, inscrutable and immortal. They don't want to see the fragility of a fellow human being who makes mistakes, gets muddled or experiences hurt and pain. Jake was the exception. He seemed eager to press me for information about my life. I probably frowned slightly, answered his questions as briefly as was consistent with courtesy and invited him to tell me his own story.

In that first session he described a peripatetic childhood with a father who was in the British diplomatic service, moving from Germany to Canada, to Cyprus and occasionally back to the UK. He said, 'It wasn't a happy time.' I asked what was unhappy about his childhood but he said some of it involved 'sadness' that he found it difficult to talk about and I should forgive him if the answers seemed a little perfunctory – and perfunctory they were. He said his mother had died when he was only eight years old and that his father was also dead. 'So I'm an orphan – and I was an only child – but you have to get through these things, don't you? Being sorry for yourself doesn't do you much good!'

I replied that many clients hesitate to speak of such private matters on a first meeting with a coach and that their reticence has to be respected. He did say that his father had been both 'demanding' and 'emotionally absent' and that there had been too many changes of school. He was bilingual in German and English with an impressive degree from a German university.

Jake had gone to the trouble of buying and reading one of my books on coaching and had done this carefully enough to have picked out a few of my more opinionated comments. He was keen to discuss them with me.

'I'd be happy to talk about that some other time, maybe, but today the focus is on you so it's my turn for the sleuthing,' I said, again steering the conversation back to his career path.

'Looking at your CV,' I continued, 'you've moved around a lot, often no more than three years or less in any one job, so I'm curious. Tell me what the thread is that joins all this up. That can often be a lot more obvious to the person than it is to someone just reading it cold.'

Jake described taking his time to find what he called his 'true vocation'. There was a break of nearly two years in his CV and he explained that he had 'gone travelling' as a thirty-eight-year-old in Asia and South America, something he dubbed 'a very late gap episode, made easier to do by being single and fancy-free – as I still am. I've had several long-term relationships . . . but I haven't met the right woman yet!'

The second session was devoted to debriefing the psychometric questionnaires. The lazy way to do this is to let computer software do the work for you but the resulting copy is usually bland, much garlanded with the cautious modifying words that will protect the owners of the software from being sued. I prefer the time-consuming way, which is to labour over the scores yourself, creating a unique narrative. When you do this, inconsistencies can be explored, correlations puzzled over and an in-depth picture of the person can emerge.

When I was still in training to use one of these questionnaires, we were encouraged to extend our learning by administering them to people we knew well. One of my guinea pigs was someone I considered to be a close colleague. To my dismay she seemed to emerge through this questionnaire as a person with exceptionally low impulse control, troubling levels of anxiety, a fierce need to be in charge along with various other behavioural features which, when combined, could suggest a propensity for solving problems with violence. I had no idea what to do with this beginner analysis, wondering if I was over-interpreting, a danger we had been sternly warned against during the training. Only two years later this woman relentlessly stalked her ex-husband, vandalized his car, sent anonymous and terrifying threats to the new woman in his life and attempted to take her own life. These and similar experiences have shaped my beliefs about the power of psychometric approaches to identifying human personality. The best of them are more or less fake-proof and give consistently reliable results.

I was puzzled by Jake's results. On one of the three questionnaires, I rechecked the scores. I had never seen a set of results that seemed so odd. He had scored at the maximum on the need to control other people's agendas and zero on those measuring how much we need to belong to a group, to accept leadership and to give and receive love. On the second questionnaire he looked at first glance to be the sort of stable, super-confident extravert that many organizations seek. At the same time this also seemed to be someone unusually calm in a crisis, a risk-taker who wanted excitement and to have his own way, unmediated by conscientiousness or by consulting others and working in a team. My third choice was a questionnaire that focuses on the shadow side of personality, aiming to identify what lies behind the social mask. The idea is that strengths can become weaknesses if they are overused; if they are seriously overused they can become career derailers. Here Jake had high scores for flamboyance and narcissism and also for the type of boldness that is associated with having an inflated view of your own gifts along with an inability to learn from mistakes.

Jake was sceptical and serious at the session where we discussed all of this.

'I don't recognize myself here,' he said. 'Sure these are my results? Could there be a mistake in the scoring?'

I assured him that however else these scores were 'wrong', it was not the scoring that was at fault. If they were inaccurate then either the human interpreter – me – or the design of the questionnaires was probably to blame.

'Ah well,' he said quickly, 'I heard a BBC Radio 4 programme recently where I think there was a lot of doubt poured on how accurate all this stuff is. The expert in the programme talked about how threadbare it was, all psychobabble. But I guess you won't agree . . .'

'No, I don't think it's psychobabble,' I said, 'but I have to acknowledge that there are hundreds of poor-quality psychometric questionnaires out there. None is perfect and they can all be affected by invisible biases, by mood and by a degree of faking or self-deception on the part of the person filling them in. The ones you did are as good as it gets where these kinds of factors are concerned. They're pretty reliable.'

I added that in my report to Harry I would faithfully note Jake's own reservations while summarizing my findings and comments.

A week or so after this I had an email from Jake. An American author who had written a bestselling book with some tangential relevance to coaching was on a tour of the UK and visiting a number of literary festivals to promote his latest book. In the brief discussion Jake and I had had about coaching and my own books, I had expressed admiration for this writer's work. Jake said that, thanks to an earlier job, he knew the author's agent, and had persuaded the writer and his agent to accept an invitation to dinner between various speaking events in the UK. The purpose was to make an introduction to me as a fellow writer whom they might enjoy meeting. The email ended, 'I hope you're as excited about this as I am and I'm keeping fingers crossed that you're free!'

Coaches are relaxed about meeting clients socially. Even so, I should probably have taken a far more rigorous view than I did, but curiosity and the chance to meet an admired writer got the better of me. I reassured myself it was as much a business meeting as a social one and that therefore there was no ethical problem.

The venue was the Wolseley, a Piccadilly restaurant right next door to the Ritz Hotel. Originally a glamorous motor showroom and after that a bank, it has marble floors, extravagant pillars, lofty ceilings and much well-polished brass and mahogany. It has confidently reinvented itself with a faintly ironic take on Britishness, is known as a haunt of celebrities and for its jaunty interpretation of traditional British and European food.

When I arrived, I found Jake sitting alone and looking crestfallen. He said he'd just had a text from the agent. 'It's taken them forever to get away from the Cheltenham Festival and they've cried off, many apologies etc., etc. So disappointing! I'm so sorry. But never mind, we can have a pleasant dinner – it's always fun at this place because you never know who you'll see.'

We were on the final course where we had both ordered a British classic, the airy, berry-filled dish known as Summer Pudding. The conversation turned to whether or not a client could become a friend.

'Not really,' I said. 'It's essential to be friendly, but friendship is something different. I have some former clients who have become friends, but only after the coaching was over.'

Jake persisted. 'I can see that coaching is potentially quite intense,' he said. 'And by the way, I'd be really interested in asking if you'd be my coach if I get the job.'

I murmured some kind of noncommittal reply.

'Surely,' he went on, 'there must be examples of coaches who have become involved with their clients?'

There is a section in my book that Jake said he had read where I write briefly about the dangers of exploitative sexual entanglements between coach and client, pointing out that such moral lapses are rare in coaching. There is no power differential between the two people: the essential precondition in which any kind of transgressive relationship of this sort is created. This is unlike the situation in therapy where the client is far more likely to be vulnerable. There may be particular dangers where the therapist is a man and the client is a woman. The evidence points to this breach of professional ethics as being more or less exclusively a problem where the perpetrator is male. I point out in my book that a typical scenario for a very small minority of therapists may be this: the therapist secretly doubts his own sexual desirability; he then exploits the defencelessness of a client who in her turn projects unrealistic fantasies on to him. Or an insecure and unhappy therapy client believes that her only gift is sex. The therapist sees her vulnerability and exploits it. I reminded Jake of this section.

I said, 'If a client does appear to be becoming inappropriately attached to the coach, most coaches would know that this is about the coaching relationship, providing data about the client's difficulties in the rest of their lives, and nothing whatsoever to do with the supposed irresistible attractiveness of the coach. In practice I've never found that this is a problem.'

There was then a brief discussion of the closeness that can develop in a coach–client relationship. Despite this, I said that boundaries in coaching were a lot looser than they were in therapy and that most therapists would never agree to meet a client socially, in other words what he and I were doing.

'Yes,' said Jake, leaning towards me and fixing me with a solemn look. He reached for my hand. 'And I'm so very glad we are. Perhaps we can be the exception to the no-involvement rule.'

Inside I froze. On the outside I doubt my expression changed much. I quietly withdrew my hand and said calmly, 'There are no exceptions, Jake.'

The waiter was summoned and I was soon on my way home.

Shortly after this I contacted Harry's office to say that I had finished the first part of the work with all three candidates, would send in my reports and was ready to embark on the second phase where I would observe each of them in their own environments. Harry was 'unavailable'. Instead I had a message to say that he would be grateful for my summaries, but that the next stage was cancelled because the selection process now had to take place at speed. I was disappointed and puzzled. Despite more phone calls and emails, there was no further information to be had and no comment on the material I had provided.

About three months later I went to a well-attended lecture for coaches given by the organizational psychologist Paul Babiak. It was called *Snakes in Suits*, the title of the book he co-wrote with Robert Hare, a criminal psychologist. The subject was how people with a psychopathic personality seduce, manipulate and destroy colleagues in organizations. Dr Babiak made the point that while all serial killers can be assumed to be psychopaths, not all psychopaths are serial killers. Psychopathy is not a mental illness. It cannot be 'treated' because psychopaths see nothing wrong with their behaviour. He estimated that psychopathy occurs in managerial populations roughly three times as often as it does in the general population. This is because the psychopath's abilities are superficially similar to many of the qualities associated with modern leadership, for instance, charisma, articulacy, persuasiveness and decisiveness. They can simulate 'empathy' without being able to experience it. They can talk convincingly about 'teamwork' but the only team they can be part of has one member: themselves. At their worst, they may inflate their qualifications and forge references. They understand human vulnerabilities. The true psychopath lacks guilt or remorse and is motivated by a wish for power and excitement. They groom by manipulating near-truths and feeding the people Dr Babiak calls their 'Pawns and Patrons' with plausible narratives. Many of these turn out to be lies. They often flout the law. The psychopath likes new-style organizations because these lack the bureaucratic controls that could find them out. They exploit the trust and gullibility of those around them. We do not expect to meet such nakedly ugly behaviour and for this reason often do not see it even when it is in plain sight and we are its targets.

The lecture was received with an odd degree of silence. I guess many of us there were thinking, as I was, about when we might have encountered a psychopath and could have been an unwitting victim. I remember feeling thankful about the extreme unlikelihood of anyone with psychopathic tendencies showing up as a coaching client when, according to what we had just heard, such people see absolutely no need for personal development.

In the same week, I was emerging from the shower at the Pilates studio and saw Sara in the changing room. She looked a little flustered to see me.

'Sara,' I said, 'you've got to tell me what happened. What explains it? Come on. Was it me? Did I offend someone? Tell me, please! I'm not going to melt away with horror.'

Even so, I listened with alarm as she haltingly told me that Jake had gone to Harry with the story that I had propositioned him during a very expensive dinner which I had somehow pressured him to accept. Gosh, he had been reluctant to do this because it was crossing coach–client boundaries. But he had felt sorry for me, a sad widow, probably temporarily unhinged by bereavement, and no doubt exceedingly lonely. It was tremendously discomfiting for him. For a start, there was the twenty-five-year age gap! He had brought the whole evening to a tactful halt. He had suggested to Harry that I could no longer be considered a reliable guide to the appointments process and that it would be better to end my engagement with the company. Though disbe-lieving at first, Harry had reluctantly accepted that this was wise advice. Harry had felt too awkward to raise the subject with me.

Jake had been appointed. Despite being the cause of a recent crisis which he had ascribed to 'a combination of bad luck and unforeseeable circumstances', he was now the hot candidate to succeed Harry himself in due course.

I found myself unable to speak for what felt like a considerable amount of time. 'Let me think about this,' I said quietly, strug-gling to contain rage and embarrassment. 'I need to be certain that I'm not overreacting in anything I say to you now.'

The next day I called Sara and asked her to take her phone to a place where she could not be overheard. I told her what had actually happened: the flowers, the oddness of the results on the psychometrics and the subtle attempts to subvert my inter-pretations, the deflecting of my questions into the details of his CV, the strangely unconvincing 'sadness' of his childhood and current circumstances, the non-appearing American author, his proposition at the Wolseley.

I said, 'I know this probably seems weird, but I strongly sug-gest you look into his CV, starting with his degree, then checking back on what he has given as his last three or four jobs, for instance, their titles and the length of time he was there. Either be your own detective or hire someone else to do it. If it's all as he claims, then everything is fine apart from my own fury. If it's not, then you and Harry will have to decide what to do.'

Sara sounded dubious. I pressed on. 'Given how long you and I have known each other, how likely do you think it is that I would have behaved as he has described?'

There were a few seconds of stillness. 'Very unlikely,' she said. 'And,' she blurted, 'I think he's a slimeball. He told Harry something nasty and totally false about me because I think he'd decided I was no longer useful to him. He seems to be isolating Harry from the rest of us.'

Jake blustered his way past the first stage of Sara's investigation by presenting her with a degree certificate and blaming the university for having 'chaotic systems' when she informed him that they had no record of his degree.

'I realized you were right,' she told me when describing some weeks later how the story had developed. 'I needed a professional sleuth because I'd stopped believing anything he said and I thought he might be too clever for me.'

The private investigator quickly discovered that Jake had enrolled at the German university but had lasted only two years before vanishing without explanation. His degree certificate was a forgery. One of his referees did not exist. He had worked in the companies listed as the most recent jobs on his CV, though in more junior roles and for shorter periods than he had described. He had been fired by one of them for reasons which they refused to disclose. His father had not been a diplomat but had served in the British Army, so his story about living in Germany, Canada and Cyprus could have been true. He was not single nor an only child. What he had said about the death of his mother was true, but his father was still alive.

During his short time in the new role Jake had made a catastrophic gamble, a carelessly considered decision, which had cost the company a lot of money. Jake was dismissed for gross misconduct and disappeared. Harry had contemplated suing him for fraudulent misrepresentation but the company did not want to lose face by admitting that its governance arrangements had been so flabby.

Individuals are always more than their 'syndromes' and 'disorders'. I believe that 'psychopathy' is just one, albeit extreme, response to feeling unaccepted and unsafe in childhood and that psychopathic behaviour is created by experience rather than being a genetic destiny. Much later, I thought that Jake's description of an emotionally sterile and demanding father had probably been true. The merciful part of me imagined a small boy whose way of defending himself against a wasteland of bereavement, sorrow, neglect and abuse had been to realize how adept he was at inventing seductive lies.

In the literature on what are alleged to be 'corporate psychopaths' there are descriptions of colleagues who had some kind of visceral response to what later turned out to be psychopathic behaviour and who were not fooled by synthetic charm. Perhaps I was one of them as each time I had met Jake I had felt a sharp churning in my gut, an increased heartbeat, a reluctance to meet his eyes and a wish to be anywhere but in that room with him. I did not like him, only half believed a lot of what he said. Although barely acknowledged to myself, I was unmistakably experiencing fear. I had set these feelings aside as unprofessional and flaky: my first mistake. What we describe as 'instinct' or 'intuition' can be reliable when it is interrogated carefully by asking ourselves: What am I noticing here? What is this based on? Is it real evidence? Had I asked myself those questions, the answers would have been that, yes, it was reliable.

When his other tactics had failed, Jake had skilfully reeled me in with the prospect of meeting a well-known writer whom he knew I admired. I had certainly believed at first that this was a genuine meeting and yet was somehow not surprised when it had failed to happen. When I discussed this whole episode with a colleague, she expressed amazement that someone like me who, as she flatteringly said, she believed to have 'a well-honed bullshit detector' had been taken in as far as I had.

Even if it was true that my bullshit detector was well honed, what I had not seen at all was Jake's probable motivation, the determination to undermine me when his attempts to exploit my supposed weak spots had failed and where a negative report from me might conceivably have thwarted his ambitions. It simply never occurred to me that I could be the focus of such calculated duplicity. It did not cross my mind until so very late in the day that I was dealing with someone who could have psychopathic tendencies, even after hearing a lecture in which those very behaviours had been unequivocally spelt out.

Such people can consider themselves to be experts in human psychology. However, they also tend to be careless. They can't be bothered with too much of the detail. This was the case with Jake.

When he mentioned the BBC Radio 4 programme on psychometrics, I didn't believe for a moment that he had heard it. If he had he would have known that the 'expert' in that programme was me and that far from condemning these tests as 'psychobabble' I had praised them for the insights they could provide. That was a warning signal. In my report to Harry I had suggested that Jake might not always have reliable judgement, even though I had no idea at that point just how unreliable he actually was.

Some people are not coachable because they have no wish to change or because their problems are too entrenched for what coaching offers. Mutual rapport and respect between human beings is fragile and easily destroyed. For coaching to be successful, coach and client have to work as equals, each has to be undefended, as vulnerable as the other; we have to take each other on trust. The focus of this assignment was assessment. My intention was to carry it out in a coaching style helpful to the participants as well as to the boss. It was not coaching as such. However openly its purposes were described, however sweetly and lightly it was presented as 'developmental' for the candidates – and it was so presented – there was no getting away from the fact that I was acting to some extent as their judge. At the same time, my own trust was abused, but then it is fair to say that I had not trusted Jake either. When one party does not behave authentically in these one-to-one professional relationships, it will trigger inauthentic behaviour in the other. The sessions become stilted and lifeless, in this case a charade culminating in the stagy performance at the Wolseley.

This was a failed project in every sense. It failed for me, it failed for Jake, it failed for the other two promotion candidates and it failed for Harry, my actual client. What I should have trusted was my instinct that something was seriously wrong. Like the old-fashioned journalist investigating some sexual scandal, I should have made my excuses and left.

Fitting In

I had never heard the term 'Andersen Androids', the all-too-accurate in-joke used by staff at the then all-powerful international consulting firm Arthur Andersen. Nor had I heard of the apparently cosy way the firm was referred to by its employees and suppliers as 'Arthur'. If I had, it would have been no surprise to be told that, even on the surreal little campus miles from anywhere just outside Chicago, full business dress had to be on parade at all times. Women were instructed to wear what was described as 'tailored dresses with a matching jacket' or if (the sniff of disapproval was unmistakable) such women insisted on trousers, these had to be in the same dark cloth as the formal jacket with a simple tailored shirt in white, pink or blue underneath. Sneakers could be worn during the permitted hours of exercise. At all other times, women had to be shod in 'heels', which needed to be at least an inch high. I had no clothes of this type in my closet. I rarely wore dresses and felt too protectively about my feet to wear high heels. Grudgingly, I took myself to a shop where such items could be purchased. I hurriedly bought a dark trouser suit just a fraction too big and at a price that made me gulp, then, just as hurriedly, some plain pumps with as low a heel as would fit the criteria.

Despite this, I was flattered to have been asked to join the faculty on a programme whose aim was to broaden the skills of senior tax and audit specialists at Andersen so that they became more comfortable with a general consulting role as business advisers. This was not a trivial issue. Disputes had become ubiquitous between the accountancy arm of the company and the vastly more lucrative consultancy branch: jealousy, resentment and bitterness prevailed.

There were forty participants and six faculty involved in this course, forty-two men and four women. I was the only British woman. When we administered a particular psychometric questionnaire, it remains the only time in my career that I have seen 95 per cent of a large cohort with the same psychological profile. These people did not want to be there. They showed their hostility openly, seizing every opportunity to question the need for the programme and to challenge the expertise of the faculty. What did we know about tax and audit? Furthermore, we no doubt earnt paltry sums compared with their millions. In the opening icebreaker, many boldly described themselves as 'independently wealthy'. Perhaps this was why they had travelled First Class to the venue while we humble faculty had been assigned to Economy.

The campus had a strangely puritanical air. There was an eight-station shoe shine parlour but the bar did not open until mid-evening. The bedrooms were monastic cells with hard little beds and skimpy curtains. I spent the week homesick and lonely. Snatched phone conversations with my children left me in tears after the gruelling slog of ten-hour days. With years of experience as a facilitator, coach and trainer, I knew something was wrong, but not what it was. From these participants I felt the intense weight of their indifference. I felt foreign. I had no idea how to navigate through ways of speaking, dressing, acting and thinking that I struggled to understand.

I was out of place, that was for sure. But who does fit in? Who gets to decide whether you are acceptable or not? The need to belong has been essential to our survival as a species. When we first emerged as a species 200,000 years ago, those who could fit in had an evolutionary advantage because they did not have to operate alone. We are, and always have been, herd animals. At the same time, we have a profound need for autonomy and individuality. Balancing the competing needs for dependency and independence can be tough.

*

Some years after my experience with Andersen, in my role as assessor for a coaching qualification, I was observing a session given by a coach who was just finishing his initial training. This young man was a coaching natural: he was pleasant without being ingratiating. He created easy rapport, he knew how to clarify the client's goals, he asked powerful questions and could subtly balance support with challenge; he created an energizing and friendly climate.

His client, Leo, was a well-paid manager of about his own age preparing for a demanding job interview, a potential promotion, where he would be facing a selection panel, only one member of which knew him. Leo was feeling unhappy and frustrated with his career. He said he had outlived his love affair with his current job and was fully ready to move into a more senior role.

This was the third two-hour coaching session in a series of four between Leo and his young coach. The goal was how to get through Leo's coming interview successfully and the session was set up so that chunks of answering practice questions were, at Leo's zealously made request, interspersed with feedback.

The coach offered positive reinforcement on the crispness of Leo's answers to questions that would probably be asked in the interview, on his enthusiasm for the possible new role, on why he wanted it and on the engaging way he was able to describe his skills. The coach also – bravely, warmly and skilfully – offered some negative points on sensitive subjects. He pointed out that Leo was wearing a suit and shirt, the ones he had proposed wearing for the interview, that were clearly well past their best. He said he noticed that Leo had dandruff on his shoulders, that his hair had descended towards his collar and needed cutting.

None of this should matter because it is all superficial. It should be possible for people to dress any way they like without being penalized for not adhering to any particular norm. I have many times heard selectors, if challenged, privately justify themselves by saying that this matters a lot. They will say that someone

whose appearance is dishevelled might have a dishevelled attitude
to their work and may lack self-awareness in general. They will
say that someone who does not use 'received pronunciation' may
convey a sense that they are uneducated or unintelligent. They
will deny that they hold such attitudes themselves, alleging that
unnamed 'other people' will object. This is why job interviews
are really about a question that is never asked: *Are you one of us?*

All of these topics were thoroughly explored in the coaching
conversation – and Leo was appreciative. 'This has been wonderful,' he said, 'so useful. I feel far better prepared for the interview
and hugely more confident.'

In the informal chat after the session, I thanked Leo for letting
me sit in, explaining again that it was an important stage in this
coach's professional development and part of the formal assessment to become qualified.

'If you wanted to take that appearance stuff further,' I said, 'I
would recommend an in-depth consultation with an excellent
image coach. She combines super-reliable judgement on these
matters with kindness and directness. I've taken many clients
to her over the years. They've all said how terrific she is and
how her advice has helped them reconsider what kind of a match
there is between what they want to convey about themselves and
what they are actually conveying. It's never mechanical, never
a one-size-fits-all process, it's closely geared to what that client
wants and to what seems to be acceptable in the organization
they want to join, so it varies a lot. We all probably have at least
a few blind spots about this. It's absolutely your choice whether
you take any notice of her advice, but I have to say that most
people do and they comment on how much difference it's made
to their confidence. They usually get positive feedback from colleagues, too. If you're interested, I could come with you. I offer a
similar service myself as one small part of what I do as a coach,
but watching her at work is like being at a masterclass. I get such
a lot out of it.'

Leo's eyes widened. 'I'd love to do that,' he said. 'Sounds amazing!'

He went ahead, contacted the image coach and took me up on my offer to go with him. The session started with a discussion of men whose style Leo admired. 'I like your choices,' said the coach. 'They all have a kind of easy elegance. Let's look at how they're doing it.'

There was then a detailed discussion, looking at photographs, identifying how, exactly, these men achieved the unforced stylishness that was such a noticeable feature of the way they presented themselves to the world.

The image coach explained that it was not necessary to go to Savile Row to get the same effect. She said there were ways of choosing a suit at the upper end of the high-street range – she named the brands – where you would get distinct improvements in quality. She said that these differences would pay off as an investment. She offered samples of good and poorer quality suiting and shirting so that Leo could handle them and assess the differences for himself. She encouraged him to see how striking he could look if he emphasized the many advantages of his tall, slim figure. She made the point that when you are bidding for promotion you need to dress as if you are already at that level.

'How do the most senior men in your organization dress?' she asked.

The answer was that they were opting for a significantly more formal look, more closely tailored clothing, darker colours, brighter ties. Leo took part eagerly in this discussion, agreeing that he could see the improvements that better cloth and a more thoughtfully calculated fit would produce.

The coach moved to an analysis of which colours would enhance Leo's eyes, skin and hair. She made suggestions about suiting, shirt and tie colours and gave him a handy-sized wallet containing swatches so that he would have an easy reference point when shopping.

'I'm surprised,' said Leo, 'just how much difference the right colours make: I can see it for myself. I look healthier and livelier somehow!'

The image coach did not hold back from suggestions about Leo's hair.

'It looks like a bit of a no-style style and you've let it grow quite long,' she said. 'You need a different cut to enhance the shape of your face. The way you have your hair now doesn't really look contemporary, and I can see that you have a problem with dandruff. But there are solutions. I'll give you the name of a salon where they have expert stylists who cut men's hair well and they also specialize in scalp problems. They cost more than your average barber, but I've suggested them to a lot of clients and they've all been enthusiastic about the results.'

I walked back to the Tube station with Leo and asked for his comments on the session.

He seemed exuberant. 'I'd have to splash out a bit on new things,' he said. 'And the cost of a decent suit was a bit of a shock. I don't like shopping and I'm out of touch! But I found it really interesting and enjoyable. You were right. She knows her stuff.'

A few weeks after the session with the image consultant, Leo had returned for his final session. I asked the trainee coach how it had gone. He reported that Leo was wearing the same suit, still had dandruff, his hair was even longer. The interview had taken place and he had not got the job. Leo was bitterly disappointed. His coach was disappointed for Leo. I was too.

If I had not seen these sessions for myself I might have assumed that this talented trainee and the style expert could have made a number of familiar mistakes. They might not have clarified the client's motivation. They could have neglected to explore the implications of doing nothing. They might have failed to create rapport, to solicit the client's views or to offer positive feedback. They might have been chilly, giving the more negative feedback too abruptly, too harshly or too vaguely. Or possibly they might have concentrated too much on the negative, raising the client's resistance. It is easy to come across as patronizing, a know-all adult talking down to a child. In my own view, none of this had been the case. There had been humour, directness and respect in both sessions and on both sides.

Leo might have failed the interview for any number of reasons, but the chances were that his self-presentation was part of the problem. When asked what had got in the way of replacing the suit and the haircut, his reply was, 'too busy'.

Leo was still committed to coaching as a way of making his next career move and his organization generously commissioned a further programme. His impressive qualifications and experience were well represented in a pithier CV. He was shortlisted for a desirable job again and was one of two candidates in the final selection process, which in this case had involved an allegedly 'informal' meal with the CEO. Such events are never really informal: they are yet another way of assessing the candidate, this time on the basis of their ease at a social event. Once more Leo did not get the job and once more both his coach and I felt disappointed on his behalf.

Organizations mostly can't be bothered to give helpful feedback to an unsuccessful candidate. They have lost interest. In this case, the CEO took the trouble to call Leo to say that the other candidate had had what he called 'more polish'. 'You were a really strong contender for this job. But I didn't think we could put you up in front of our senior clients unless you had a bit of a makeover,' he said. When clients are faced with such humiliating feedback, I have encouraged them to make their own decisions: do they want to be pragmatic and conform, or do they truly feel it is far too trivial to matter and they can live with the consequences?

My training work with Leo's coach ended and I had no way of knowing how any of this was explored in their further sessions. But over the years I have met many examples of the same phenomenon. For whatever reasons, the client cannot or does not change the behaviours or social signifiers which, however unfairly or irrationally, are probably standing in the way of promotion. Sometimes they minimize the importance of the feedback they have had, seeing it as inconsequential. Sometimes, especially with women, there is profound fear of looking foolish. As one client said, 'I can't bear to look as if I'm trying too hard and scared of getting it all wrong, or of not really understanding the hidden rules, so it's better not to try at all.' In some cases, clients have told me they feel they will be showing disloyalty to their parents or region of origin if they change their way of speaking.

Perhaps Leo's dread was of seeming inauthentic. He had grown up in a London borough with one of the highest levels of social deprivation in the UK, was the first in his family to go to university and the first in his school to go to Oxford. One client quoted the example of the late Cecil Parkinson, a senior government minister when Margaret Thatcher was prime minister. Parkinson began life as the son of a railwayman. His agonizingly drawled English public school accent and perfectly groomed appearance seemed to some to suggest the mighty effort that went into concealing his working-class Lancashire origins, not helped perhaps by revelations at the height of his career about the betrayal of his long-time lover and his initial refusal to acknowledge their child. 'The man was a fake,' said this client. 'I'm not following that path.'

Prejudice can be subtle, disguised as a rational reason for rejecting a candidate for an elite job. Employers will say, as in Leo's case, that they are looking for 'polish'. Research has shown that this is a proxy for people who share humour, accent, family history, leisure pursuits, school, university, dress. I openly raise the topic when I encounter people like Leo in my own work. We will discuss *code switching*, the useful concept from linguistics which means being able to move effortlessly from one mode of communication to another. I think here of a client with a Nigerian father and Irish mother. He was the only one of his four siblings who did not work in a service or manual job. He had a social work background and was now in an influential role. He had me laughing helplessly while he demonstrated his impressive ability to match Nigerian family members, then to be totally different with the Irish branch, different with old mates from school and different again with colleagues and politicians. This was not just different vocabulary and syntax but four different ways of using his body and face. He took it for granted that this was entirely natural and extremely useful in his job. He saw nothing inauthentic in it. Such seamless switching is not for everyone, nor should it be, but it is one way to steer through the dense thicket of cultural complications.

On my way home from Heathrow after my stressful trip to Chicago, I took a call from the distinguished professor who was the lead consultant on the Andersen project. He told me that my services were no longer required for the rest of the planned extensive programme with the firm. I asked for the reason. He was a kind man and I could hear him hesitating. 'They thought you were a bit too British. Too low key. I'm sorry. You didn't really fit in.'

There was probably useful learning for me in this episode, but whatever it was remained opaque as I was never able to extract more information about my failings. I received the news of my firing with maybe a few seconds of hurt pride and indignation, along with fleeting regret for what would have been substantial fees. Within moments I realized that I was freed from the heavy burden of many more trips to an environment I had found so sterile and with people whose company, try as I might, I could not enjoy.

Only a year or so later Arthur Andersen were accused of large-scale false accounting as auditors to the disgraced US energy company Enron. They were found guilty of criminal complicity. Andersen closed their tax and audit business and started a new consulting life as Accenture. When organizations fail there is rarely a single cause, but I have never, before or since, met an organization so clearly in the grip of Groupthink. This concept was developed by the social psychologist Irving Janis to describe the way that groups can create rigid and often fatally damaging barriers to any questioning of their collective thinking. People who challenge are enemies. Psychological fences are reinforced by narrow bands of acceptable attitudes, signified in dress, gender, age, education, social class, ethnicity, nationality and sexual orientation. In their open boasting about 'Andersen Androids', the senior people at Andersen genuinely believed it was a competitive advantage to recruit and encourage clones.

I had left the Andersen campus thankfully at the end of that miserable week. A taxi had been ordered for me. We drew up at O'Hare airport. I had been instructed not to tip, as 'Arthur' had already paid in advance for the journey. I hoisted myself out of the spongy seat and handed the young woman driver my last dollars as she lifted my case out of the trunk. She had been silent throughout the journey, answering my attempts to make conversation with a quick shake of the head and, 'Don't speak good English.'

She acknowledged the tip with a tiny nod. She gave me a luminous smile then pointed to my heeled pumps, still pristine.

'Nice.' Our eyes met for a moment. 'Can I have?'

Wordlessly, I nodded. I shook my feet out of the shoes and handed them to her. 'Wait a moment.' Fumbling to unzip my suitcase on the sidewalk, I tugged out my sneakers, hastily squashing my feet into them.

'Would you like this as well?' I touched the jacket and mimed shrugging myself out of it.

This was how it came about that I made the long flight home, definitely lacking 'polish', a little shivery, wedged into my Economy seat, in the unflattering white shirt, the formal trousers and the sneakers. As I closed my front door behind me, I stepped out of the trousers, threw off the shirt and stuffed both garments into the bin. Never again.

In balancing our need to belong with our need for individuality, we may sometimes conclude, as Leo may have done, that the price to be paid for acceptance is too high. The dropout rate from Andersen's graduate scheme was substantial, perhaps for the same reason. Today, it may be that employers are having to question the narrowness and commercial cost of their assumptions about who is 'in' and who is 'out'. This has become a sensitive subject when campaigns like #MeToo and Black Lives Matter highlight the systemic bias invisible to many of those who are sustaining and benefiting from it.

My own efforts to fit in with the Andersen culture were half-hearted and nothing truly important was at stake for me in my failure other than short-term loss of face. For clients like Leo, the stakes can be higher – a whole future direction. His seemingly baffling refusal to change his appearance was also a reminder that it is the client who makes the choice because it is the client who has to live with it, not the coach. I remind myself of Leo and clients like him when training and supervising other coaches, and in my own work. Neuroscience has shown that the human brain prefers the status quo, even when the status quo is uncomfortable. At least the discomfort is familiar whereas the benefits of change are unknown because we have yet to experience them. When faced with the need for change we sometimes tell ourselves that if we don't try, we can't fail. The effort can seem like a gamble. Or we contemplate success and the thought of it is terrifying: it may seem better to stay safe with what we know. Or the change may confront us with a challenge to our core identity.

This is why we may realize that the problem is not with us as the individual, it is with the organization and its deeply embedded prejudices, seamlessly reinforced in its systems and processes. People who have profited from them may naively believe their success is down to their own ineffable talents rather than to the luck of having been born into the right class with the right money, at the right time, with the right contacts and knowing the right codes for success. When these codes have to be learnt as an adult, it can feel as if you are always playing a part, ever vigilant in case someone sees underneath your disguises. Faced with this choice, we may subtly, and sometimes not consciously, make it clear to those judging us that we are rejecting them so that it is easy for them to reject us. When we don't want to pay the psychological price of joining that seemingly desirable club, there can be enormous relief in stepping away and saying, 'No thanks, not for me.'

Fragile

Executive coaching is expensive. The people who get it are mostly those at the top of organizations where the size of the fee can be justified by the supposedly massive impact the client can have on the organization. Every now and then a generous boss, often someone who feels they have greatly benefited from coaching themselves, will sponsor coaching for a promising junior.

This was what happened with Tamzin. Still only in her early thirties, she had been singled out for superstardom. I took a call from the HR director in her London law firm.

'She's incredibly bright – double first at Cambridge and all that, got through her training contract brilliantly, qualified in record time, can get across a complex brief so easily. We want to keep her for the long term, we need brains the size of the planet and that's what she's got. We've just promoted her and she's having to manage a small team of other lawyers for the first time. We could send her on a management course but we feel that coaching might be a better route.'

'What's your thinking there?'

'She's quite sensitive – you know, a bit like a racehorse – very unusual, needs careful handling. We think she'd do better solo than on some kind of course, and we think she'd do especially well with someone like you.'

Did I notice the flattery implied in that 'someone like you'? Did I wonder whether a person who was being described as 'sensitive' had it in them to be a boss, where some degree of prudent *insensitivity* is essential to do the work? These ideas should certainly have been somewhere in my mind and alerted me to possible danger, but were they and did they? I was intrigued by the idea of adding this famous law firm to my client list and of getting to understand how it looked from the inside. I liked the idea that the potential client was considered to be 'clever' and that I might be considered clever enough myself to work with her. Did it occur to me that maybe other coaches had been considered, or even approached, and had been rejected or possibly had done the rejecting? If any of this went through my mind, I must have suppressed it.

I do remember the lengthy pause that followed my question about this potential client's *sensitivity*.

'What do you mean by sensitive, exactly?'

'Err . . . Well, she can get a bit upset from time to time so one point of the coaching might be to help her deal with that.'

My guess is that eagerness to bind this illustrious firm more tightly to my client list overwhelmed any sensible signs that there was more to this young solicitor's problems than there appeared to be on the surface. Perhaps this is too harsh a judgement on my less experienced self as I have worked successfully with many clients subsequently whose sponsors have been equally vague in their hints about what might really be going on for the potential client. But I did observe my own informal rule that an initial conversation was essential. The point of this conversation is to check out how good the fit is between what the client wants and what the coach offers. Tamzin sounded wary. She talked a lot. She complained about her new role. She said she was overworked and underappreciated. She described her own brilliance, mentioning her academic achievements. Then, with chilling and fluent scorn, she set out her distrust of the whole idea of 'management'. This was nothing new to me as I had been hardened to professional cynics from my coaching work as a member of the BBC's staff and subsequently as a coach to many BBC people. It was taken as read that anyone who was a *manager* was by definition overpaid, added no value, and was so chronically dull and untalented that they had been unable to make it in an editorial role.

Tamzin's comment was, 'They say I'm some sort of manager, but my real work is the legal business and all that management guff is just rubbish, isn't it?'

Inviting the coach to collude with the client in some kind of invisible battle against the organization is a blind alley. Coaching is a balance. Whatever is going on, the client will be contributing to it in some way. You are a neutral outsider, yet you always have the client's interests at heart. At the same time, a client who makes this kind of comment, knowing that the coach is someone who specializes in management issues, may already be subtly implying that the coach herself is as useless as the ideas she explores through coaching. At that stage I ignored all possible negative interpretations, saying, 'Well, we'll have to explore how far that's true when we get together.'

I came away from that phone call with a faint sense of anxiety but folded the unease away into some inaccessible place, reminding myself that I knew next to nothing about this client and that it was too soon to judge.

Tamzin was thirty-five minutes late for her first appointment. This was a striking woman. She was wearing the lawyer's black business suit, but it was obviously expensive, worn with a bright-red silk shirt and toweringly high heels. Her hair was modishly cut, her make-up immaculate with a slash of crimson lipstick. Her handshake was limp, puzzlingly at odds with her dramatic appearance. She avoided eye contact as we made our way to the small basement room, the only one available in the offices I was using at the time. I profoundly disliked this room. It had a low ceiling and noisy air conditioning, and a well-meaning designer had made an attempt at simulating daylight by installing a large neon-lit panel. This meant that there was always some dazzle wherever you sat. One of my clients from the Metropolitan Police had joked that the room was fine by him because it reminded him of what he called the 'interrogation chambers' familiar from his work. This was despite the fact that, at six foot five inches, he had had to be careful to avoid bumping his head on the ceiling as he came in.

Unless there is some major problem on the transport system in London, it is rare for a client to be more than a few minutes late. Tamzin merely mumbled something that was not an apology and, still not looking at me, said my directions had been unhelpful and she had wasted her valuable time trying to find me. It was true that the numbering in this street was a little eccentric but our standard directions were, I thought, clear enough about how to get around the confusion.

How many people meeting a professional contact for the first time would start the relationship by failing to apologize for being conspicuously late and then blaming the other person for their lateness? Not many. I was startled and felt an instant prickle of hostility.

Unasked, Tamzin plunged into the story of her childhood. The confident lawyer disappeared in that first session as she described her family life. She said she had grown up feeling that she was unloved and unlovable. She said that as a small girl her older brother had sexually abused her but when she complained to her mother she was told she was making it up and was punished with slaps. She described beating, hair-pulling and verbal abuse from both parents as being a routine part of what growing up had been about. At the same time she said she had been told in public that she was special – specially bright, specially pretty, specially cute – and indulged with specially expensive material gifts. She described a family obsessed by status and money, gracious in public, punitive and cold in private. When she was ten years old her father took a job abroad and Tamzin was sent to a famous boarding school for girls. She wept as she described her sense of having been banished, her loneliness, her alienation from the other children. They rejected her, she said, because she was prettier and cleverer than any of them.

This story was so terrible and told with what seemed like such well-rehearsed theatrical style that I found myself wondering how much of it was true. It is rare but not entirely unheard of for an occasional outlier client – they never last more than a single session – to recount appalling and extreme stories, often involving satanic abuse, kidnapping, famine, torture or fires. I have come to be wary of such stories, having found later in several cases that they are the delusions of people with serious mental health problems. Nonetheless, as so many stories of childhood abuse now confirm, I reminded myself that the starting point should always be that the person is telling the truth, however difficult it is for the listener to hear.

This part of the conversation had been continuing for about forty minutes when Tamzin suddenly stopped. For the first time she looked at me properly, but it was to glare with anger.

'This room is horrendous. I can't be in it. I can't hear myself think because of the noise from that air con. And I feel the walls are closing in on me. It's hateful.'

'I'm sorry. I don't like it either, but it's the only one available today. Would you like to stop or are you okay to go on till six o'clock?'

Scowling and twisting in her chair, she agreed to continue.

We talked about her new job. Like many professionals who may not be especially attracted to a management role, she had accepted the job, given to her without competition, because it was a promotion and this meant more status and more money. Her eyes glittered as she told me what her salary was: it was generous, a lot of money for someone of her age and career stage. Her understanding was that her job was to do exactly what she had been doing previously only on a larger scale. This meant working on bigger projects where more was at stake for her firm.

Managing her team was an irrelevant irritant. 'They should just get on with their jobs.'

How was it then that these people were showing every sign that they were not doing their jobs? That they were making mistakes? That they seemed surly and uncommitted? Tamzin told me about her own time as a trainee when, she said, she had many times stayed all night to finish some work, sleeping under her desk. 'I did that and all young lawyers should be prepared to do it if they want to get ahead. It goes with the patch.'

At five minutes to six I glanced at my watch and said we would have to stop. Tamzin's eyes filled with tears again. 'But I still haven't told you about my idiot boss.'

'That will have to wait till next time – assuming, that is, that you want a next time. We really, really do not and should not go on with this if you are reluctant.'

'Oh yes, please don't say you won't work with me!'

It was a pleasant evening in late spring and I was glad I had brought my bike to work. Cycling home would allow me to simmer down and consider what to do next. How could I work with a client whose mood changes were so bewildering, who aroused hostility in me that was unbecoming to a coach and who also aroused profound pity, neither of these healthy features of any relationship? And, most of all, a client who was so evidently a candidate for therapy?

The newer a coach is to coaching, the more worried they are likely to be about some supposed boundary with therapy. As I have become more experienced I have blurred these allegedly rigid boundaries, mostly because I don't really believe in them any more. Even so, it is obvious that there are clients who need something different from coaching, either in addition to or instead of it. Coaching assumes that people have a sense of agency – in other words, they accept that they are responsible for themselves and that they can act to affect their own lives.

The symptoms that this is missing include persistent distress, inability to recover from past trauma, outbursts of unmanageable emotion, intrusive thoughts which affect daily necessities like sleeping and eating plus threats to harm yourself or others.

I arranged an emergency phone call with my coaching supervisor, vital for situations such as this where I had no idea what to do. Should I just terminate the coaching straight away? Should I suggest therapy? What was this saying about me?

Her advice was to continue but to concentrate on the managerial aspects of the agenda and to challenge rudeness with neutral feedback. She also suggested that at some level it was likely that Tamzin would get value from our sessions.

I arranged to talk direct, with her permission, to Tamzin's boss as her sponsor for the work. This man was another young lawyer, also recently promoted and who cheerfully confessed to knowing little about being a manager. The phone call was notable for its blandness. He was concerned about what he described as her *stress*. When I pressed him for examples of how this stress showed itself, he struggled to reply. 'She just gets a bit agitated.' What was his advice for her? 'She should chill,' he said. 'She should learn to delegate – she's got some good people around her. She doesn't need to do it all herself.' I had wondered whether Tamzin gave way to crying and tantrums at work but after asking some cautiously worded questions that might have uncovered this, it appeared she did not. Her reply to me when I had asked her a version of this question was, 'I'm very nicey-nicey at work. I'm just being honest with you,' so it seemed this was true.

Tamzin cancelled our next session at a few hours' notice and at the same time pressed for an early alternative. 'I'm desperate. I need to see you,' she said. The only available room in our offices was the same dismal dungeon to which she had objected so violently previously. Stifling my concerns about the cost, I booked a room with a local company specializing in letting pleasant, neutrally furnished rooms at hourly rates.

It began badly. Once again, she was late. Whatever desperation she had been feeling had evidently evaporated and she launched herself into an attack on one of the two psychometric instruments I had given her. 'I spent a long time on the internet looking it all up. I see that most decent psychologists think the whole thing is rubbish. It's all just bollocks, isn't it? I don't know why you thought it would be useful. And I found a lot of online articles attacking them and saying they were outmoded.'

I daresay my jaw actually dropped at this statement. It was confrontational, it was wildly inaccurate, it was astonishing that someone who complained of being chronically overworked had spent so many hours gathering material whose entire purpose seemed to be to undermine me. With the safe distance of time, this episode gives me a wry smile. I had paved the way for the provocation myself by telling Tamzin that I was the author of books on both of the questionnaires I had asked her to complete.

At the time, I stared at her, amazed at her rudeness, held on to the need not to match rudeness with rudeness and said something like, 'After recommending that you might take this questionnaire, you won't be expecting me to agree.' I was probably frowning and conveying at the very least disagreement and most probably disapproval as I said this.

Tamzin cringed. Her tone changed instantly. She said she would defer to me, would do anything as long as I agreed to go on working with her. We discussed her results on the psychometrics. We stopped for a cup of tea.

There were thirty minutes of the session left.

Now I had recovered some equanimity. But it was no use continuing until we had discussed what was so obvious: that this relationship was not going well. 'How do you think we're getting on?'

I left the silence unfilled for what felt like a long time. 'Do you really want to go on with this coaching? If you don't, we don't have to, and I can't work with a client who doesn't want to be here.'

'Yes, yes, I need this! I need you! I need to be able to talk management-talk and you'll help me do that.'

It was a moment of despair for me. Did I really want to go on with this problematical client? No. But nor did I want to give up on her. I said, 'We can only work together if there's respect between us. This means that as your coach I need to feel you respect what I can offer and that I respect what you bring too. It can't work if we're engaged in constant wrestling matches about who is right or if you don't turn up or if you cancel at short notice. I will find it upsetting and if I'm upset I can't be what you need.'

'Please, please don't give up on me. I do value this, honestly I do.'

I raised the question of therapy. I said we could continue with the coaching but it would need to concentrate on the managerial competence that she needed to do her job. I talked about the distress and emotional extremes she had shown in her conversations with me and told her I did not have the experience or skills to help her but that the right therapist would. Meekly, she agreed that she had often wondered if therapy could help and we briefly talked about how it might do so. I gave her three trusted names and the details of a website where she could find more. As we parted, she avoided eye contact yet again and the phrase *slinking away* came to me.

After another helpful conversation with my fellow coach I realized that the only way to continue coaching this client was to provide strict boundaries: no more compromising over rooms, no more cost-free cancellations, no more phone conversations outside the sessions, no more ignoring lateness without challenge, plus quiet confrontation of aggression, explaining how and why it was unacceptable. My colleague also told me to anticipate that Tamzin would probably reject every one of the therapists she contacted.

And so it proved. Each had something wrong with them. One was 'too dim', one 'too schmaltzy', one 'too rude'. I wondered especially about the one who was 'too rude': had this man perhaps challenged some of the behaviour he would undoubtedly have heard on the phone?

Somehow we struggled through the remaining four coaching sessions. The first one was devoted to discussing her most pressing immediate worry. This was a complicated case concerning intellectual property where she described hating the work she was doing, spending many hours on research and feeling overwhelmed by the responsibility, saying that vast sums of money for her firm's client were at risk. The people from the client organization were 'stupid' and did not seem to understand how they had created all of their problems themselves. We explored some ways of managing the stresses, though Tamzin claimed that she had already tried all of them and none worked. Once again, I felt her message was, *See, there's nothing you can say or do that will help me*, and that perhaps a more effective coach would have handled the discussion better.

In most organizations, however competitive the culture, help is available, and the more there is at stake for the organization, the more likely it is to be offered. I suggested we look in detail at our next meeting about how to delegate at least some of her work to others in her team and how to ask for help from seniors. I knew one of these seniors. A kind, generous man, he had been a client when he was at a different firm. Without revealing how I knew him, I said, 'How about approaching Martyn G – he's done this kind of work, hasn't he?'

Her reply was instant. 'Oh no, he's far too senior and a bit haughty, so I couldn't possibly ask him.'

Each subsequent session was devoted to further mutually agreed aspects of being a boss that Tamzin was finding difficult: for instance, how to influence seniors, how to chair and be a member of a meeting, how to give a presentation. There was one outbreak of hostility where in response to some topic or other she burst out, 'This coaching thing is ridiculous. They [her firm] are crazy to pay you for this.' When once more calmly offered the chance to end the coaching if she was not finding it useful, she again retreated.

The rest of the time, Tamzin was docile. She arrived on time. There were no more last-minute cancellations. Reviewing the whole programme at our final session, she said she had found it *useful*, a word that despite my pressing for more detail remained vague. She even said she would ask her firm for more coaching though I had already decided that if this were to happen I would find a way of saying no. Normally I enjoy keeping in touch with clients through occasional emails. This time I felt relief as I said goodbye to her and was aware that I had no interest in encouraging further contact.

It would be easy to have remorseful regrets about this whole episode or to wish that I had never agreed to do it. Still troubled by it, I presented the case to a discussion group of fellow coaches. One member was a psychiatrist as well as a coach. 'Oh dear,' he said. 'You were working with a classic Narcissistic Personality Disorder – and they are just so manipulative!' This led to a lively debate about whether people with personality disorders could be coached. I was silent during this discussion because I was preoccupied with wondering how helpful it was to categorize people as a 'disorder'. To me, the dismissive label 'manipulative' is just a word for influencing tactics that are a comprehensive failure. People who are described as 'manipulative' do sometimes get what they want in the short term but always at the cost of destroying the liking and respect of those around them. I concluded there was some comfort in seeing that her behaviour fell within clearly recognized patterns, and in understanding that she was unable to find any stable image of me as her coach. In her head I had probably seemed to vary between some kind of mother figure who would nurture her, a critical parent waiting to trap her or a remote expert who would pronounce on her.

Despite my earlier doubts, in retrospect I feel sure that Tamzin's account of her abusive childhood was substantially true and that the person I saw in the coaching room had brought me some version of a 'survival self', a protective shell of see-sawing, dysfunctional behaviour which, in her case, had become pitifully disabling. I was clear then and now that I never saw the true Tamzin during this coaching. The healthy self that lay somewhere beneath her disconcerting mixture of boasting, craven begging and fear was never present and perhaps never could have been, given that her real and most urgent need was skilled therapeutic help.

My discussion with fellow coaches did not resolve the ethical dilemma of whether to take on someone as vulnerable as Tamzin as a client. A number of events can trigger the request for coaching: someone whose opinion they value criticizes them harshly, a relationship fails, they flunk an important professional exam, they make a business decision which proves ill-judged. In Tamzin's case, my guess is that a promotion had triggered the dread that she would be exposed and humiliated.

Sometimes these dreads combine with a pervasive fear of intimacy and there is no one in their immediate circle who can help them when the crisis occurs. They need intimacy because they feel so emotionally deprived, but they drive people away with their overwhelming demands. These same emotions can mean that they intensify the way they perceive the human failings of those around them. Discrimination and harassment are real and continuing problems in organizations. To people like Tamzin, profoundly hurt and damaged, ordinary feedback or requests to complete work can become bullying; a smaller bonus than they wanted can become discrimination; their own excessive outbursts are misunderstood. They can easily see themselves as neglected or marginalized.

Threadbare though I feel the actual coaching was, maybe it was some kind of an achievement that she kept coming to the sessions. I heard nothing more from her. About eight years later at a social gathering I met someone from her firm and tentatively enquired after Tamzin.

'Oh yes – gosh, she crashed and burned,' he said.

Did I somehow spot a smirky glint in his eye as he said this?

Tamzin had had what had been described in public as 'a break-down', but this had disguised a series of outbursts where she had accused a number of her bosses of bullying. She claimed they had deliberately piled work on her, so much so that it was impossible to complete, and that all of this had caused a serious depression. This had resulted in several weeks of sick leave. The firm had a whole division devoted to employment law so they knew how to head off the disaster of an employment tribunal by negotiating an agreement. Tamzin had been paid a large sum of money to go away quietly.

Clients like this remind you as a coach that real change is complex. We have to be willing to challenge our excuses about why we can't do it. Coaching will fail unless the client can take at least some responsibility for themselves, including seeking therapeutic help when it is one of the best options for healing. At some level Tamzin knew full well that she needed to change and that she needed therapy, but the idea of changing was terrifying. Her tragedy was that she did not believe that anyone, including me, was up to the challenge of helping her, and she was correct in this: I was not up to it.

Tamzin had poked with expert recklessness at my wish to be an authoritative professional. To protect herself she had found my own fragility, she had drawn out my own survival behaviour to the point where I had temporarily lost the ability to be engaged yet detached, to be authentic, the state of mind that is essential for effective coaching. My energy went into protecting myself. Clients like Tamzin stretch your confidence to its limits.

They resurrect old weaknesses. They remind you of your own necessary fragility. Carl Jung espoused the idea of the 'wounded healer': 'it is his own hurt that gives the measure of his power to heal'. Unless you are conscious of your own weakness and able to manage it, you cannot work with others on theirs.

Undressed

As Nicholas strode through the door, a strong smell of stale tobacco surged in with him. I noticed straight away that his collarless shirt was unusual, that he was wearing vaguely non-Western clothing and had a substantial moustache at a time when they were distinctly out of fashion in London. He gave me a warm grin and shook my hand vigorously, saying, 'I'm told that if anyone can sort me out, it will be you!'

My company had won a bid to provide coaching for people who had been designated 'at risk'. This international organization employed British and American executives to run their global operations. A sharp decline in revenues had led to much manoeuvring at the top and a ruthless CEO from outside the company had just been appointed. His emphasis was on rapidly reducing headcount, improving efficiency and cutting costs. A layer of management jobs had been deemed unnecessary and our clients had been brought back to London and told they had to compete for whatever jobs were now available. With the apex narrowing so sharply at the top, such jobs were in scarce supply and the appointments process was tortuous.

Nicholas was in his middle fifties and had spent more than half his working life in South Asia. He had a reputation in the company for being a talented and individualistic public performer, able to tell anecdotes with flair and humour. He was well known in the country where he had most recently worked. He and his Indian wife had five children, some of them still young enough to be in full-time schooling.

Most organizations with global operations limit the time their executives spend in any one place. They tend to move them ruthlessly around the world with no more than three years in one place. The aim, as one HR manager firmly told me, is 'to prevent them going native, because if that happens they're bugger all use to us'. Nicholas had skilfully circumvented this policy. Rather than doing as almost all his colleagues did, which was to take advantage of the organization's offer to pay for boarding school education in the UK or US, he had opted for the local international schools. When asked to change countries, he had often been able to point out with charm and patience that there was at least one child at a critical stage in their education and who could not therefore be moved without immense psychological and educational damage. He told me proudly that his children were trilingual and added that the youngest two had 'slightly Indian' rather than British accents. I already knew that Nicholas spoke fluent Hindi and Urdu.

The reason the appointment with Nicholas had been arranged so hastily was that he had been shortlisted for yet another job, with the interview just a few days ahead. Interview coaching can be distinctly different from the usual run of executive coaching. If the client has been shortlisted for a job that they really want, then often all they need is a single two-hour session. There is also less time for the niceties of getting to know each other unless the interview crops up in the course of a longer programme. The coaching has a brisk, transactional feel. Clients usually stress that they want you to get to the point. Nor do they come for the coaching out of some fluffy feeling that it might be a sort of helpful thing to sort of have just in case. Much more commonly there is a pattern of previous failure: repeatedly getting turned down for jobs that should have been well within their grasp. When this happens it cannot simply be explained by having been the victim of incompetent interviewing or a prejudiced panel. This may be a plausible explanation the first time, but not if it recurs.

Just occasionally, especially if an internal promotion is involved, clients will have been given skilfully offered, specific feedback. Much more commonly they will have been dismissed with soothing platitudes such as 'the candidate we appointed just had the edge on you' or frank lies. Interview panels are increasingly timid about what they say to the candidates they turn down, perhaps out of fear of being sued.

Nicholas had been rejected four times for jobs on exactly the same level as his previous role and had no clue about why. With an intense edge to his voice, he told me that he was hurt and angry.

'I've worked in this organization for a long time and I've worked hard. My results have always been good, we've met our targets, I've created strong teams wherever I've been and I know I'm popular with my staff. The executive team say they want talented leaders and that's what I am. I feel my track record has been thrown back in my face. I've always had a decent bonus, but I've seen less experienced and less good people appointed to jobs I could have done with ease. I felt I'd done well in the interviews and I know I made them laugh and they seemed to give off positive vibes. When I've asked why I didn't get these jobs I've been fobbed off with stuff about how I was appointable but the other guy was a bit better. When I ask in what way better I just get a circular answer, it's maddening.'

Job interviews are often presented as rational affairs with weighted lists of competencies and elaborate scoring systems. These are sensibly designed to prevent what actually happens most of the time: instant irrational decisions made on first impression and prejudice. When you are in the role of interviewer, you mostly cannot help making your choices on the basis of whether you warm to the person and whether or not you could imagine working harmoniously with them.

Corporate life asks for conformity in behaviour. I was familiar with the dress code in Nicholas's organization and had seen it change during the time I had worked with it. In earlier days it was a little louche – a degree of hipster *je ne sais quoi* was the norm. If you dressed too formally it was a sign that you were unsophisticated and insecure. A change of ownership had seen this casual attitude replaced by something different. When the most senior men began wearing expensive suits with elegant shirts and ties, the other men were swift to copy. A degree of quirkiness was encouraged in the choice of tie: bright colours and witty symbolism were acceptable, as long as the tie was a brand with cachet. 'Dress Down Friday' meant chinos, linen jackets and pricey button-down shirts.

I asked Nicholas what he planned to wear to his interview. He pointed to the clothing he was wearing.

'This – or something very like it.'

'How does that compare with what you see your senior colleagues wearing?'

'Huh – they look like tailor's dummies, all of them. I'm not dressing like they do!'

'May I offer you a different view here?'

'Yes of course, as long as you don't expect me to agree.'

'When you make a point of dressing in an obviously different way from the way your selectors are dressed, it's like saying that you don't value them and their customs, or see yourself as one of them. It's giving them an excuse to reject you. It's up to you, of course, but how far do you want to take that risk?'

'You should feel free to be yourself without pretending,' he replied. 'Appointing someone should be about whether they can do the job, not about whether they're wearing the right tie – and by the way, I never wear ties, they're an outmoded piece of Victorian tat; I feel strangled in them.'

As he spoke he waved his arms about vigorously and did some self-throttling slapstick.

What about the tobacco smell? There are few ways in which it is acceptable to offer social criticism now that expressing prejudiced opinions on ethnicity, religion, sexuality, gender and age have been officially outlawed. But it is still possible to disapprove openly of smokers. This coaching took place before smoking was formally made illegal in any public place in the UK but the trend towards regarding smokers as deluded idiots who were a danger to themselves and others was already well established. It is obvious if a client is one of these pariah addicts. They almost always have one last cigarette before entering the premises. Few of them seem aware that in a smoke-free environment where virtually everyone is likely to be a non-smoker, the smell of tobacco is instantly detectable. It was more than this with Nicholas. His skin, clothing and hair were probably all permeated with tobacco. Was it possible that no one had mentioned this to him since his return to the UK?

I knew that it was all too possible. What happens is that it seems too personal and everyone hopes that someone else will do the deed. What can be more embarrassing than telling someone that some aspect of their personal hygiene is offensive? This is why it so often falls to a coach to raise it and the coach cannot afford to be as pusillanimous as everyone else.

I said, 'Nicholas, I need to mention something to you that I've noticed because this may be at least one part of why you're not getting anywhere with your interviews. Is that okay?'

'Well, yes, of course, but what?'

'As you came in I noticed a really strong smell of tobacco and I can smell it now. And I can see a lot of nicotine on your fingers. Are you aware of it?'

Nicholas flinched. He said that he was not aware of it. He bravely asked, voice strained, how bad it was. A friend would be fearful of damaging the friendship or causing hurt and would probably draw back at this point, offering false reassurance on the lines of *no, it isn't that bad, just a little bit bad*. A coach is not a friend but nor is it easy to say what others have avoided. I bit my lip but pressed on. I said it was noticeable to me so others would probably notice it too, so yes, it was 'bad'.

Smokers have to become experts in deflection when pleaded with by their friends, their doctors and by children who have been well warned about the dangers of tobacco at school. To be a dedicated smoker in the UK is now extremely unusual when you are in a professional role. It has become largely a habit of the poor and marginalized. To smoke is another way of declaring yourself to be different. Committed smokers who do have professional jobs are fully conscious that they are regarded with patronizing pity by colleagues and rarely attempt to justify their addiction. They will anticipate questions about giving up or would-be helpful tips about how to do so by telling you of their plans to do just that – but not right now.

Giving people advice about something they already know they should be doing is hopelessly unlikely to result in that person humbly agreeing and changing their behaviour. Before being trained as a coach and learning the self-discipline of avoiding advice-giving, I had been married to an enthusiastic smoker for many years. I had tried every useless tactic for persuading him to stop. At the time of writing, both my sons are smokers, something I find agonizing to watch. Yet as a coach one of the first skills you must learn is that your well-meant desire to rescue clients from themselves is counterproductive. No one in the UK smokes because they are unaware of the health risks.

There was a thoughtful silence. Nicholas cleared his throat.

'Wish I could have a puff right now!'

'Well, you can – this is a non-smoking office, but it's a nice day and you can go and stand outside if you like – I'll come with you.'

'No, no. Let's carry on.'

Nicholas explained that he had worked for decades in countries where tobacco was cheap and where the anti-smoking message had yet to be heard as powerfully as in the UK. His wife was a smoker, so was his eldest son and so were many of his staff. Somehow Nicholas had failed to notice that opinions and behaviour had changed in the UK. He had also not appeared to see that his loose, elegant waistcoat, collarless shirt and moustache looked oddly different from the clothing choices of his peers and seniors in London.

In preparing clients for job interviews, I spend what might seem an inordinate amount of time on how to give a convincing reply to the one question that is asked in any interview: *Why do you want this job?* This question is about motivation and is one of the few in a traditional panel interview that yields anything of value to selectors. It will tend to identify personal values, your inner motivation, your understanding of the organization you wish to join and how, ideally, all of this in a fabulously close match to what they need. If your reply is that you don't really want the job or are unsure, then you have lost it from that point on.

I asked Nicholas how he had been answering this question in his recent interviews.

'I've probably been too honest.'

'Too honest – how?'

In his answers to this question at the interviews, Nicholas had openly described his ambivalence about the jobs, assuming that the interviewers would appreciate candour. Three of the jobs had been London-based. He had expressed doubts about how much he and his wife wanted to live in such an expensive city with its not always pleasant climate or to send their children to London schools. He would lose his tax advantages. He was unsure about working at the corporate centre after so many years of autonomy in running his own operation abroad.

I asked Nicholas to imagine that he was the selector and that I was him, and replayed his typical replies.

'How did they land with you?'

'Ouch! No – I'd stop listening after that! I'd give the job to someone who really wanted it!'

Nicholas did not want any of the jobs he had competed for. He had entered the race because it was expected. He had at first believed that the organization was a benevolent god, managing his fate for him. It had never really been doing this, but it was true that in its earlier manifestations it had been a more pleasant place to work, with a generous, easy-going camaraderie. This had been slowly submerged over the years by innumerable mergers and acquisitions. Expecting the organization to look out for you, to notice your virtues and to behave well by you is almost always a fast track to disillusion. Many of us endow the organization we work for with mythical powers, believing that in some way it will transcend the pettiness, fears and human failings of the managers who run it. In any organization, however happy you are, it is wiser to see every assignment as short term and an opportunity for learning. It is sensible to have an exit plan, however vague, in the back of your mind. It is much healthier to understand that there is only one person who is managing your career and that is you.

What keeps us stuck in roles that we have outgrown, or that have outgrown us, is fear. We fear that our skills are trivial or not transferable. We fear that any new employer will believe we are old dogs who can't learn new tricks. We are afraid of finding out that all of this is true. And yet underneath all this fear we do know somewhere that it is time to go because we have lost our commitment. Some people work it out for themselves. Some wait for the organization axe to fall.

Nicholas and I discussed some of this.

'Well?' I asked him.

'Well . . . Maybe this isn't my place any more? What do you think? Where would I go – and I've got a wife and five kids!'

'It doesn't matter what I think but it does matter what you think. What would need to happen to persuade you to stay and to compete for these jobs?'

There was another silence. Then, 'Nothing would persuade me. There's nothing they could do. I don't respect the people who run the organization now. I don't think their strategy is right. I don't like the way they behave. I've argued against it but I can't make my voice heard. I think they're destroying the value of everything that it's stood for. I think their so-called cost savings will reduce profitability, not enhance it. They should be looking at how to increase revenue and at the underlying problems. They don't respect our traditions. I don't really want to be part of it. I don't belong any more.'

Nicholas had lost faith in the senior people running the company. Most organizations have lists of 'values' and often put such lists on their websites. These stated values may be widely upheld, like the Johnson & Johnson Credo which has been essentially the same since it was first crafted in 1943, committing to putting 'the needs of the people we serve first'. Sometimes such values are a cynical exercise in slick marketing. Unless they are spelt out in terms of what behaviour goes with them, they are meaningless. They are also meaningless if they do not act as a moral compass in times of difficulty, helping to make difficult decisions in ambiguous situations where the right course of action is far from clear. Nicholas felt there was a chasm between the company's stated values and what he saw in action. In his view the senior team considered these values irrelevant. 'They say we treat people with respect,' he said, 'but we don't. Increasing short-term profit is all that matters. Their promises are empty words. I've tried to create my own little oases but it's increasingly hard to do.'

Nicholas swiftly arranged some further sessions. He arrived at the next one telling me that to the amazement of his colleagues he had withdrawn his current job application and although this felt 'scary' it was also a relief. Our work then was to answer the questions that Nicholas had himself posed. If this organization and role was no longer right for him, then what was?

Many people in this situation ask themselves the wrong additional question: *Who else will have me?* It is usually too soon to ask this question. Much better questions to ask are about core identities, identity in the plural because all of us have many. If you are the best possible versions of yourself, what kind of person is this?

In Nicholas's answers there were themes of philanthropy, performance, language and a love of Asian culture and literature. How did these compare to the way he had actually been expending his energy? The answer was 'very poorly'. His real interests had been confined to his limited leisure hours because so much of his time had been focused on delivering results for the company.

It is always instructive to see how an organization handles dissent. Many will claim that they encourage what they call 'challenge' but few can tolerate much of it, especially when it takes the form of criticizing seniors. It is why whistle-blowers so often have a hard time and are frequently sacked, with counter-accusations about their own performance. Nicholas had argued violently against the strategy he saw unfolding. He had presented what he thought was compelling evidence that the executive team were refusing to understand local economies because they were too hidebound by what Wall Street or the City of London thought. He had pointed out that they were not behaving according to their own set of values. There seemed to have been a reckless panache about what he had said and how he had said it. When told that his opinions were unwelcome, he had refused to be silenced.

At his leaving party Nicholas introduced me in his speech as his 'Coaching Wizardess', indulging his quarter-serious fantasy that I had magical powers. Human transformations are not normally made as a result of anyone chanting spells or waving a magic wand, though for cheap effect I did for some time have in my coaching room a £5 pink plastic fairy wand that I had filched from my little granddaughter, but I was not the person who waved it. I always handed it to the client and invited them to do the magic.

Nicholas had hidden his dissatisfaction in plain sight, symbolized in his Asian clothing and his moustache. His refusal to conform had been disguised as humour, outspokenness and eccentricity. His heavy smoking had been a sign of his misery, well concealed inside an affable, dynamic exterior. He had not wanted any of the available jobs. The organization had applied pressure, I had asked a few of the critical questions. The rest he had done himself.

At our final session he said to me of his seniors, his voice thick with satisfaction, 'I saw through them. I undressed them. Underneath their fine clothing there was nothing there. Just as I said – tailor's dummies . . .'

Nicholas negotiated a generous settlement with the company. He and his wife severed their remaining links with London by selling the house they had been letting for many years. They relocated to an Indian city where they bought and refurbished a studio space which was to become a performance centre and a place for experimental drama training and workshops, intensely involved with its local community. Some of the running costs were subsidized by a part-time university job.

I watched all this through friendly emails and little snatches of action on YouTube. I saw that Nicholas was now calling himself Nikhil or Nik. His dress became more noticeably Indian. In sending me an email a few years later he drew my attention to his lack of moustache and said that a persistent cough had led to a health scare which had frightened him enough to give up smoking, something he claimed he had done 'with ease'. He added, 'Pointless to deny it, Jenny, I know how much you disapproved and I know you didn't like the 'tache, and even if you didn't say anything, you didn't fool me.'

Nicholas had been right about his former company. A few years later it issued a profits warning and was swallowed by a competitor.

Holding Hands

My potential client looked furious. She was glaring at her boss. 'Why haven't you told me this before?'

'I have,' he said, 'but you weren't listening.'

The three of us were sitting in a small meeting room. This firm was ahead of its time. They had bought a lease on a converted factory in what was then a dismally neglected part of London. Despite the grimness of the street outside, it was a visually pleasing place to work. The handsome nineteenth-century windows gave unimpeded light from several sides. There was a south-facing roof terrace with impressive cacti, there were tables and umbrellas where you could eat your lunch on a sunny day. Inside there was classic twentieth-century furniture shown off to perfection against untreated brick walls and polished concrete floors. Staff sat at their desks on Eames chairs, lounged on Le Corbusier sofas and had their meetings around Bauhaus tables.

Stella's boss, the CEO of the company, was now calmly facing her, reminding her that a staff survey had revealed her team to have the lowest engagement scores anyone had ever seen and that two of her team had recently resigned.

'We can't afford to lose these talented people,' he said. 'And you, Stella, are the link.'

'It's nothing to do with me,' she cried, 'they are too much, they're all mavericks, they resent being told, anyone would find it hard to work with people like them!'

I had already been briefed by this boss. He told me he had poached Stella from a rival firm because he saw her as a source of endless creativity. She had shaped and led projects with ideas that had won loyalty from pernickety clients and was making a name for herself in a notoriously competitive and unstable sector. He saw her as a person who would give edge to a group of creative people who had, as he put it, 'slightly lost their mojo'. Some years previously, as young graduates, he and Stella had been colleagues and friends in another firm.

'I did know what she was like,' he said, 'but I had no idea that when given this job, a big promotion for her, by the way, she would turn into some kind of raving bully. Have you heard that expression "Bully Broad"? Not a nice label, but she's it – unusual behaviour in a woman, it's normally men who get it wrong this way. She has to do things her way – or else. She's loud, she's short-tempered, she doesn't listen and she seems to think people will forgive it all just because she'll buy them a drink in the pub in the evening and tell wickedly funny stories. She thinks they'll put up with her behaviour because she's so brilliant at what she does and fantastic with clients. I'm tired of folk coming to me to complain about her and we're losing good people because they can't stand the way she treats them.'

In sounding me out, the CEO had asked what I thought was a strange question: 'You're not easily frightened?' When I asked what he meant, he said he saw it as a risk that Stella might try to overawe me with her cleverness, put me down by drawing attention to my lack of knowledge of their world, or might try the same tactics on me that she tried with everyone, flip-flopping between beguilement and intimidation. Coaching was one last attempt to get Stella to pay attention to messages he said he had already given her. This time there would be a clearly defined balance of inducement and penalty.

'We're prepared to invest in you, Stella,' he said, 'but it's not a blank cheque.' Speaking slowly and carefully, he said to her what he had already said privately to me.

'If you can change, I will offer you equity in the company, a place on the board and a fancy title of your choice. But to do this I will need to see a major readjustment in your leadership style and I'm prepared to give you all the help and mentoring you need to make that happen and to support Jenny's work with you. If you can't do it, you will have to go.'

Stella could not hide her fury. She raised her voice and told him he was wrong, wrong, wrong, look at the clients she had brought in, look how much better the work was, it was unfair and he had betrayed her. He remained unmoved, just repeating his message: change or go.

As he and I had agreed, the CEO then left the room. Now it was time for Stella and me to have a private conversation. Stella had avoided looking at me throughout this meeting but now she turned to face me full on.

'I've never been so humiliated in my life,' she said, a vivid flush in her neck. 'I thought he was my friend. I've created a mass of new work when this company was struggling, I've given them a new lease of life. Possibly I've saved them from collapse and now he throws this at me. He doesn't understand how tricky my job is. He's not even giving me the choice of coach. What is coaching anyway – some sort of soft-soap therapy in disguise? Is it all about lying on the floor and holding hands? Why should I believe you can do a thing for me? I really don't mean to be rude, but are you a Creative? Do you have the smallest clue about the world I work in?'

I was aware of being faintly amused by this display, noticing for instance that when people like Stella say, 'I don't mean to be rude,' they usually do mean to be rude. I realized I had just had a personalized display of exactly the kind of behaviour her colleagues complained about. I guessed that her annoyance would subside as quickly as it had started. I explained to Stella that she and I had to agree whether to go on. I acknowledged her anger and her feeling of having been cornered. I told her it was perfectly possible that I might not be able to do anything for her. If she wanted someone from her own professional world then she needed a mentor, not a coach, but it was my impression that she needed no help with the technical aspects of her work, the area a mentor rather than a coach would deal with. What I could help with was how to get a good performance out of people without coercion, where they gladly gave of their best and more. Her boss had made the time and budget available, but I was not prepared to role-play being her coach. If we were to continue, I would need her active assent. I said I could see how reluctant she was to accept that her poor staff survey results had anything much to do with her and that she was leading a team of talented, opinionated people, but there were known ways of managing creative people that I would be happy to share with her.

'It's like herding cats,' she said. 'They're all independent-minded and cocky, all full of themselves, it's impossible.'

I have heard this said so often by people in Stella's position that I have my reply ready.

'Actually, it is perfectly possible to herd cats as long as you have an open tin of tuna. Or go to any hotel on the beach at Paphos in Cyprus and see the packs of semi-feral cats being herded by guests feeding them scraps of breakfast bacon. And talking about inducements, how much do you want the rewards your boss is offering?'

The answer, grudgingly, was that she wanted these rewards a lot. We ended the meeting agreeing that I could possibly be her best hope of getting them, but I was fully aware we were each on probation with the other.

Energy and the certainty that you are right is attractive. You seek responsibility eagerly and employers appreciate your drive. Your propensity to be forceful in order to get things done is seen as an allowable weakness. You win big bonuses and get promoted. These assets can become liabilities when further promotion means that for the first time you have to lead others in settled teams rather than in short-lived project groups. People resist: they object to being yelled at. Increasingly such colleagues are willing to lodge formal grievances and the best talent may leave. The speed with which this can happen can leave people like Stella bewildered. Why don't the old tactics work?

I asked Stella if she would nominate eight colleagues for me to interview about what it was like working with her. Stella had already told me that she'd never heard of a single person in her sector having coaching. It was shaming. She did not want anyone in the firm to know about it; she had suggested that our sessions were covered in her diary by fictional appointments for elaborate dentistry. So how could she possibly agree to have colleagues interviewed about her? If such interviews had to happen, then how about making it something about the whole team and not just about her? I saw it as essential not to collude with this request for secrecy and reluctantly she agreed.

My report was a shock to Stella. She was taking her multiple talents for granted – her quick creativity, her ease with clients, her passion for the business, her intelligence. Many people had also described her kindness and generosity, for instance paying for an office birthday party for a nervous young intern and buying people thoughtful wedding presents. She had no idea that people found her *intimidating*, that they spent a lot of time and energy managing around her. She did not know they felt she rewarded sycophancy, thought she needed an admiring audience at all times and could not brook disagreement. She was unaware of her inability to delegate without redoing people's work, that she rarely gave praise, stridently explaining that getting results was all that mattered and that people should assume they were doing well until told otherwise; praise was for wimps. Stella was inclined to be disparaging about the skills she did not have, so dealing openly with people's disappointments and anxieties she had often described as 'wussy fluffy stuff'.

In my report I quoted three comments on her which summed up many that were similar:

'If you take her some draft copy it invariably comes back with innumerable crossings-out in red. You feel like a kid again, it's so undermining.'

'In the morning, someone always mutters, "What's the temperature today?" If she's in a bad mood and the reply is that it's icy with storms coming, we know to keep out of her way. If it's that there's a warm front, we can all relax.'

'We have a joke that she's Dr Jekyll and Mrs Hyde and you never know which you're going to meet. If it's Mrs Hyde then you say what you have to and get out quick.'

Stella was simultaneously embarrassed and intrigued. She did not lack nerve. 'I've never failed at anything before in my life and I don't like failing at this leadership thing,' she said. 'I've got to get it right. Will you come and run a meeting with me where we talk all this through with the team?'

This request was at the outer edge of what clients do to acknowledge a feedback report. A few hate the whole process so much that they assign it to an anonymous grave. Some just muse on it privately. Some give brief verbal thanks to their feedback-givers. Some give the headlines in a guardedly worded email. Very few indeed choose to do as Stella did, which was to give copies of the unadulterated report to everyone. I saw people's raised eyebrows and their snatched glances at each other in this meeting. The ones who had made some of the harsher comments looked a little apprehensive, even though I had rigorously removed anything that might identify them from my report. 'Is it really all right for us to read this?' one asked nervously.

People began to speak openly for the first time at this meeting. One pointed out that Stella was scornful of people who gave way to their emotions, for instance by crying, yet she could not control her own temper.

Stella's most pressing task was to acquire a whole new way of being a leader. She had to learn to manage her impatience when people took longer to solve a problem than she would herself, or found a different but equally viable solution. She had to learn that emotional intelligence was what every leader needs and that denying her own softer side at work was cutting her off from much of what mattered to her staff. She had to challenge her belief that you kept work and home totally separate and that what went on in people's private lives had no connection with their work. 'You mean I've got to ask them how their kids are?' she said to me, distaste in every hissed syllable.

Most of all she had to learn to listen and to ask questions without knowing the answers. She found this daunting. At one point she said to me, 'It's like learning a new language and one where I feel I will never speak like a native.' My reply was, 'You don't need to speak like a native, just well enough to understand and be understood.'

It may sound as if this work was going well and at one level it was. Stella never repeated the snappiness of our first meeting. She made ample time for our appointments, kept notes in a special folder with a huge label saying 'MY COACHING' on the outside, followed up on my reading suggestions, never did last-minute cancellations, debated everything vigorously and told me that her boss was pleased with the changes he was seeing. There had been no more resignations from her team. Yet I felt uneasy. I was aware that somehow we were not truly engaging.

At around this time there had been a bereavement in my life. My 22-year-old goddaughter, Charlotte, had contracted a virulent form of influenza which had rapidly turned to pneumonia and then septicaemia. After a month in an artificially induced coma, the dedicated staff in the intensive care ward had to acknowledge defeat: she had multiple organ failure and there was nothing more they could do. The equipment was switched off, the lines withdrawn, and she was moved into a side room. The eight of us who had mounted a 24-hour rota, a vigil at her bedside, were with her when she died, a quiet, peaceful fading away of what had been a vibrant life. I had loved and been close to her since her babyhood and found it almost impossible to accept that she had left us. In the street I would see the back of a tall young woman with the same spiky hair, androgynous clothing and assertive stride and would think for a joyous moment that it was her, it was all a mistake, she was still alive. My own children were the same age and Charlotte's death was a terrifying reminder of the fragility of human life.

I had given my clients, including Stella, a brief account of these events. I was aware that I was often operating on autopilot, that I still had the feeling of seeing myself in a film and that everything that had happened was fiction. I did faintly recognize that I was using work to bury grief.

Stella and I varied the locations for our meetings. Sometimes we met in her own office, sometimes she came to my apartment, sometimes it was in the coaching room at my offices. There was a date when we were scheduled to meet at my home. It had followed a day when I had at last given way to grief with a long lament of helpless crying. There had been a sudden change in barometric pressure and it was thundery. About an hour before the agreed time for our meeting, I felt the beginnings of a migraine. For me this is the classic 'aura' often described as flashing lights. I knew it would be followed by a severe headache. If it is really bad, my speech is affected. Mostly what we migraine sufferers want to do is lie in a darkened room whimpering until we feel human again, often many hours later.

About ten minutes into our session, I felt I needed to explain to Stella that I was in the throes of a migraine as a way of explaining that she might find me 'a little slow'. Probably I was fooling myself. My speech would most likely have been incoherent. We continued for another twenty minutes.

Stella tapped the table imperiously. 'Really, Jenny, this is ridiculous. You are unwell. You are still coping with the loss of your goddaughter. You've got a migraine. Stop pretending to be the perfectly professional coach. I'm making you a cup of tea, you're going to tell me where the painkillers are and then you're going to bed.' Briskly, she moved into my kitchen, boiled the kettle and made a single large mug of tea. I watched meekly.

'Now, are there blinds in your bedroom?'

I was speechless. Stella marched into my bedroom and pulled down the blind with efficient blackout on its outer side chosen for just these circumstances. Coming back to the table, she reached for her jacket and then pressed my hand lightly with hers, leaving it there for a little while. 'Cut yourself some slack. You are now going to bed, you are going to drink this tea and take the paracetamol and you are not to get up for at least another two hours. Okay? Promise?'

Dumbly, I nodded. I touched her hand in reply. Stella swept out. I did sleep. The migraine was over with remarkable speed.

About a month later I had a message asking if I'd be prepared to have our next meeting at Stella's home, a highly unusual request and normally one that I would politely refuse. I forget the reason. Perhaps it was explained as some kind of childcare crisis. Stella's husband opened the door with a warm smile. He tapped the side of his nose meaningfully without speaking, a mystifying gesture – did it mean 'take care' or 'this is a secret' or what? He ushered me into their sleek kitchen. Stella was there, but what was this? There was a startling change in her appearance. I was looking at a woman with no more than a few wisps of hair at the centre of her head but a normal head of hair at the front and the back.

'Yes,' she said, 'a bit weird, isn't it? I'm a baldy! But I thought it was okay for you to see the real me.'

Immediately after the birth of her second child, Stella had developed alopecia. All the hair at the top of her head had fallen out and although doctors had told her it might grow back, it never did. She employed someone whom she assured me was 'the best wig-maker in London' to create undetectable hairpieces for her. She had told no one at work and no one had ever appeared to notice.

We had a remarkably easy coaching session, punctuated by visits to my lap from the cat, snufflings for treats by the dog, offers of wine as it got towards evening and an invitation to stay for the supper prudently pre-assembled by her husband. I accepted and left much later, with hugs all round.

Stella and I finished our coaching programme, zooming through innumerable topics with energy. She still had difficulty with impatience but mostly she did now control it. When we were nearly at the end, she asked me to come once again to run a team session with her to review her progress. One of her team said at this meeting, 'Well, something has changed. When she looks as if she's about to have one of her mighty explosions of yore, she'll stop now and say, "Uh-huh, watch out, Mrs Hyde is about to come out again!"'

Stella joined the board of her company and did give herself a fancy title. She also enrolled herself on a coach-training programme run by my then company, finding it, as she said, 'jaw-grittingly hard to do – was I your worst student ever?' She hired me to do a cut-down version for her team, grinning wickedly as she said to them at the opening session, 'I know, I know, poacher turned gamekeeper, eh?'

When you work in any kind of helping role, whether as a clinician, therapist or coach, it is widely assumed that you must keep your professional distance. You are taught that it is better to be neutral, personally invisible, never to touch, never to show emotion with your patients or clients. Yet when Charlotte was dying, the single most helpful professional I encountered was the nurse who had been at her bedside for a month, was with her and with us when she died, who held my hand on that dreadful night and did not hide her own tears. That same nurse gave up a day off to come to the funeral.

You are taught as a professional about the dangers of 'transference' and 'countertransference'. You are taught to be alert to the possibilities of abusing your power, whether sexually or in other ways. You are taught to anticipate that you could cause harm by getting too personal and are shown explicitly how to create protective barriers. Your role is to be a giver rather than a receiver; a giver of rapport, understanding, acceptance.

But receiving is not a weakness. Recently, I thought one of my own doctors was looking a little strained and as I was getting up from my chair I said quietly, 'And how are *you*?' He told me I was the only patient in twenty-five years who had ever asked this question, sprang forward, gripped both my hands with his and said, 'Thank you, thank you.'

What is conventionally the most 'professional' thing to do or way to be is not always the most helpful. A touch can heal in ways that words cannot and most of us know instinctively how to do it. Simple human gestures can convey profound meaning: a pat, a hug, listening intently, the offer of a drink, adjusting a chair, arranging a cushion, eye contact, a genuine smile. Allowing my unguarded self to be cared for by my client allowed her to show her unguarded self to me. It allowed some magic to happen and I still don't know exactly what that was.

The Courage to Change

The Challenge to Change

Living the Dream

It no longer surprises me that so many of my clients, a lot of them notably successful people, had a parental bereavement in childhood. Many of the leading political figures of the present and recent past had dead, absent or alcoholic parents – for instance, Nelson Mandela and his first wife Winnie Madikizela, Barack Obama, Eleanor Roosevelt, Bill Clinton. Roughly half of the people in our prisons suffered the early loss of a parent. These devastating absences and losses could maybe drive a child either way: determined to succeed despite the challenges, or peculiarly vulnerable to temptation and exploitation.

Where did Dexter fall on this spectrum? I was uncertain, but his early life was difficult enough. He was the youngest of four children born on a housing development notorious for drug dealing and other crimes. When he was only two years old his father was killed in a pub brawl. His mother could not cope. She used alcohol to stifle her pain and seven years later she, too, was dead. Dexter described his experience flatly.

'There were some people who helped. My sisters and I used to go to a neighbour after school and she'd give me my tea.'

Somehow they had fended off social services and the threat of being taken into care.

'My oldest sister had to be my parent, but she wanted her own life and she got pregnant when she was seventeen.'

After that, Dexter was on his own, receiving the reluctant attention of an aunt too distracted by her own problems to give him more than sporadic care.

Dexter had gone to a seemingly ordinary local school but perhaps it was not quite as ordinary as it looked. Over half of the children were entitled to free school meals and it served an area of severe social deprivation. It had an outstanding headmaster who had recruited talented teachers, many of whom gave their time freely to a wide range of after-school clubs. These included music and drama.

Several of these teachers spotted something unusual in Dexter. His mathematics teacher saw his quick intelligence and told him he must aim for a top university. Meanwhile, his raw talent as a singer, composer and musician was emerging through after-school clubs. When the school put on a concert he was spotted by one of the patrons supporting the school. He never took up his place at Cambridge because by then he was in a band, signed by a record company and already on his way to success.

I am well acquainted with celebrity. In my earlier career as a TV producer, my colleagues and I had the power of patronage. We were able to find little-known experts in their subjects and spot their potential, teaching them how to work to the camera and how to write the bestselling books that typically went with our series. Not uncommonly, we saw many of these people rise to fame and considerable fortunes though, unlike the more savvy producers and directors of today, we made not a penny out of that joint success. In parallel with this, my husband had run a series of BBC departments. His work involved daily contact with household names – politicians, journalists, presenters, newsreaders, actors, writers, singers. These people, too, had become part of my world.

I have never had any interest in the world of pop music and I confess that I had never heard of Dexter. The friend who put us in touch would only say that he was facing some 'tough decisions' and needed the objectivity of a coach.

Superficially, the celebrity life is glorious. People appear to regard you with awe. As if you didn't already have more than enough desirable objects in your life, eager PR people shower you with even more in the hope that you will be photographed with their product. You eat for free in famous restaurants. You get upgrades on planes and in hotels. You give interviews and, with remarkably few exceptions, these interviews are bland and flattering. This is because any journalist who dares to write anything less than glowing will be threatened with excommunication by the PR minder who is always present.

As a celebrity you stop doing everyday things. You can't travel by public transport, even should you want to abandon the chauffeur-driven car, because people will whisper, point and ask for autographs. You can't go to the supermarket without being waylaid, but in any case, all that stuff is taken care of by the live-in housekeepers who do the cooking. You can afford a stylist to choose your clothing and you may become afraid of choosing for yourself. You dare not go out without your full rig: perfectly groomed hair, immaculate face, stylish outfits, even on a private beach in the Caribbean, because you will for certain be 'papped' either by the long lens of a professional paparazzo or by the multitude of amateurs ever eager with the cameras on their phones.

It takes an extremely mature person to cope with all of this. Young celebrities such as footballers and singers are especially vulnerable. Often they have been spotted, as Dexter was, while still teenagers. They are told that there is no point in finishing their education because they won't need it. Powerful substitute parent figures such as managers and agents persuade these unformed young people that they are special. They begin to move in the world of other famous persons because they are told that only the famous understand what the celebrity life is like. There is truth in this because when you are a celebrity, people stop being able to relax with you. They giggle foolishly, get tongue-tied, squirm helplessly when they talk to you. No wonder celebrities speak of 'ordinary' people as 'civilians'.

This is the tipping point. A PR myth has been created around you because this is what earns the money for the army of experts who are there to support what has now become your 'brand'.

Sometimes these people skilfully separate you from your family and original friends. If you are a performer, you also have to deal with the adrenaline high of hearing the rapturous applause of large audiences. When that evening is over, you don't want to go to bed. You want the high to continue. You need time to come down. You begin living your life backwards, hiding during the day, coming alive again in the evening and night, demanding that people stay up with you, maybe drinking and taking drugs, and they do because they want a little of your celebrity to come to them. Alcohol and drugs are particular snares if you have seen addictive behaviour in a parent. People are constantly pursuing you because of your status, money and fame. The wife of a famous actor once told me that even in his late fifties when his looks had faded, young women would shamelessly approach him, including times when she was present, pressing their phone numbers into his hand. You start believing that the rules of good conduct don't apply to you and that you can behave as you like; it doesn't matter if you hurt people or exploit them.

Some of this had happened to Dexter.

Is it any surprise that so many people caught in this system do know they are living a lie? The false front, what Carl Jung called 'the Persona', is an intolerable burden. Elvis, the glorious voice and beautiful young man, dead at forty-two, stuffed with drugs and junk food. Princess Diana, vulnerable and manipulated, dead in a car crash pursued by the very paparazzi she had cultivated so carefully. Michael Jackson, inconsolably lonely, an insomniac whose doctor administered the surgical anaesthetic which would bring sleep when nothing else could and which killed him. In all these cases their deaths were a direct result of their fame.

No wonder celebrities self-medicate with alcohol, painkillers and sleeping pills as well as suffering anxiety attacks, depression and a high rate of marital breakdown. After the intense exposure, performing as the high-octane version that your public has come to expect, you crave oblivion, you want to escape from the false self you have become.

At our first meeting, Dexter seemed a slight figure, bespectacled, modest, the kind of person you could pass without a second thought in London. He arrived helmeted and anonymous on an ordinary folding bike of the sort that so many Londoners have because we are, quite justifiably, ever wary of having our bikes stolen by one of London's many dedicated bike thieves. The fact that Dexter and I owned the same model in the same colour was a small moment of initial bonding.

Dexter told me about his early life and the intense feelings of abandonment he had experienced as a child.

'I felt that if only I'd been a nicer, better kid then my parents wouldn't have died and I wouldn't have had to scrabble around begging for care from my aunt who never really wanted to add me to her household because she had kids of her own, and I was always second best.'

Human beings need autonomy and with it the bravery to take advantage of what it might offer, including the risk of making mistakes. The need for autonomy is accompanied by its twin, fear: fear that we will take autonomy so far that we will be alone and, at its extreme, abandoned. Our second great need is to be accepted and loved unconditionally, the shadow twin of which is our fear of being smothered, engulfed, swamped. When, for whatever reason, a parent has disappeared, the fear of abandonment and the belief that you are not worthy of unconditional love can become overwhelming, a need that can sometimes only be met by surrendering to people who have their own exploitative reasons for appearing to love you.

Dexter's career appeared to have stalled. He had fallen out with his most recent agent. His early commercial success seemingly could not be repeated, his marriage was failing. His large tax bill could only be paid with a struggle.

We did not spend a lot of time on these dismaying facts. Dexter had a realistic grasp of what had happened to him, though the idea that his early life had preconditioned him to accept the exploitation of agents, managers and producers seemed to be new.

'I always saw myself as a survivor.'

'Indeed, that is exactly what you were.'

'And I was needy – but I couldn't look at that, it was too painful.'

'Yes, it must have been. So it was painful and you were a survivor. And you do have those needs. And you found ways of getting them met.'

'At a cost.'

Dexter's immediate question, and the reason our mutual contact had suggested coaching, was that he had been approached about appearing in a TV reality show. These shows, allegedly involving 'celebrities', are almost always about attempts on the part of the contestants to revive a flagging career. No current A-list celebrities ever appear on them because they don't need to. Would you want to eat kangaroo testicles or ants in the Australian outback, to risk the humiliation of trying to dance when you always knew that you were physically clumsy, to take part in ridiculous party games in a pretend house in East London, if you did not desperately need to get back into public consciousness? Only one person can win these contests. Even when the judges or voting public are generous with their comments, all but one of the contestants has to leave, rejected and quickly forgotten once more.

On the face of it this was a relatively small decision, barely big enough to merit the time and attention it had been allocated. I was intrigued to know what it was that made it so significant. Sometimes we seem to be standing at a fork on our life paths. The decisions are more painful than they look. They represent something that hurts and the hurt is big enough to get our attention.

I asked Dexter what made this such an important decision for him.

There was a long pause before he answered, 'I suppose it's what to do with the second half of my life.'

The second half of life is often about recovering from the poor decisions, evasions, missed opportunities, pointless sacrifices, follies and indulgences of the first. When the grey hairs begin to show, when the wrinkles are not just the short-term effects of too many late nights, then we have to ask ourselves whether we want to continue in the same old way. Yet the lure of the familiar life is still there and our hope can be that any feelings of failure and disappointment are just temporary. I have worked with many clients who believed that a wrecked relationship would repair itself, that a departed lover would return, that a boss who had failed to offer a promotion would admit his mistake, that the cancer diagnosis was a mix-up, that the latest in a long line of failed auditions would be successful, that a dying business would magically recover.

'What's holding you back from answering that question?' I asked.

'If I'm not the person I've become, then what am I?' Then, 'What gifts do I really have? Who am I?'

This is an especially troubling question for people whose worldly success seems to be out of proportion to their talent. Many people could read an autocue competently if they had the chance, many people can write stories, many people have decent singing voices and can entertain others with acting and performing, yet very few become celebrities through the use of these skills. Those people who do become famous may sooner or later question whether what they have achieved is down to their own talent. They ask themselves how much they owe to the many others – producers, directors, managers, corporate executives, editors, sound engineers, publicists – who have treated them like a product to be relentlessly promoted.

Dexter's crossroads seemed to encapsulate a dilemma that was distressing and pressing. Was he finished, washed-up? Was he fated to open suburban supermarkets and appear in pantos, as he said, 'at places like Milton Keynes', a town notorious for being a bland 'new town' no longer new?

We always know what is right, but the task of stepping into the unknown, into that risky arena where we can grow and develop, can seem terrifying, especially in the face of repeated setbacks and insults to self-esteem. The path silently but persistently asking to be taken will nearly always mean leaving what has been known and familiar. The price of refusing is high: the terrible unease of knowing that we have repressed what truly matters. Yet the more important the choice, the more we pull back and hesitate.

It is easy to see why it might be hard to turn your back on the celebrity life. But at the very height of your fame, the same system that has created the myths is preparing to destroy you. Whatever the reasons – resentment, envy, spite or just the natural processes of change – your world begins to crumble. Your manager or agent tells you that you need plastic surgery to stay attractive, but then when you follow their advice, you just look 'young' in a strangely odd way. Rivals appear who are allegedly more talented. Spurned lovers or, even worse, spurned family sell their stories to the tabloids. 'Escorts' set honeytraps. Whole magazines and internet sites are devoted to celebrity 'disasters': looking fat, scowling, falling out with a lover in public, being clearly drunk during a night out, doing cocaine in a club, a few inches of cellulite visible, an unfortunate choice of clothing at an awards ceremony, being photographed kissing a same-sex buddy when you have consistently denied being gay.

For all that your public wants heroes and heroines in their lives, they do know you are mortal and flawed just as they are. When people see you close up, they cannot help noticing that you are somehow shorter, scrawnier, fatter, older, scruffier, the roots of your dyed hair showing, balder, with stumpier or skinnier legs, more heavily made-up than they imagined. In so many ways you are less perfect than the Photoshopped image they are used to seeing.

Dexter had played the part of young star to perfection, but it had lost its glitter for him and for his public. He clearly did have talent, but it was not my role to give him a professional assessment – he knew plenty of people in the music business who could do that.

Dexter had many personal qualities, quite different from the plastic personality created for him by the PR machine. His true strengths included persistence, a commitment to fairness and equality, creativity, entrepreneurial flair, psychological insight and generosity. We spent one whole session looking to assess not what his talent was but how he might identify and then use these character strengths on finding answers to the issues that haunted him.

A fellow coach who also works as a therapist in LA once told me that trust was the biggest hurdle in working with his many famous clients. The celeb has realized that almost everyone in his or her life has a stake in keeping things just as they are. But once trust has been established, the coach can become the one person who can challenge and suggest boundaries because a coach can walk away freely. In fact, oftentimes the celeb may need the coach more than the coach needs the celeb. 'Even so, it can be hard,' says this coach, 'but now and then you just have to say, *Look, you're going nuts. Your life is in pieces. Stop it.*'

Speaking hard truths may sometimes be necessary, but as a coach you have no stake in what the client should do. You are unattached to their decisions at the same time as you are keenly interested and hopeful they make the ones that are right for them. There is no need for fancy tools and techniques. The best coaching is about asking powerful questions, not about having smart answers. Even so, some clients are searching for a guru and my refusal to play that role, despite being paid generously for my time, can sometimes exasperate or upset them. 'Couldn't you tell

me what to do or even just ask me a closed question for once?'
asked one client tartly. I usually explain that any answer I give
to the problems that clients bring would soon prove to be limiting and that the process of my giving it would be undermining
and disrespectful. Our own answers are the ones we really hear.

I asked Dexter some further questions.

'What else is going on in your life that could have a bearing
on your decision?'

'What part have you played in creating the situation you find
yourself in now?'

'What are the upsides of saying yes?'

Then, 'What are the downsides?'

'What would be the consequences, the obvious and the unin-
tended, the long term and shorter term, of following any one of
those paths?'

Years ago, people in the oil industry, facing troubling organizational choices, all of which appeared to have major disadvantages,
coined the phrase 'standing on the burning platform' to describe
these alarming dilemmas. The rig is on fire, you can't stay on
it; the idea of jumping into the sea is appalling. Yet denying the
impulse to jump will mean certain death. Almost all major decisions in life will involve a 'death', a giving up of something we
have prized or that has defined us, even when this defining is distressing and limiting. There is a strange comfort in its familiarity.
It is impossible to make the transition without acknowledging
what has been lost, mourning it and then being able to leave it
behind, accepting at the same time that the future is uncertain,
challenging and unknowable.

We had this discussion. It was quiet, thoughtful, difficult,
extensive.

Dexter left with the main question unresolved. Being on that
reality show could mean the revival of his career, a new lease of
life, but was it worth the gamble?

★

At what was to prove to be our final session, Dexter swept into my apartment, snatching off his helmet and impatiently folding his bike.

'I had a dream,' he said, 'and you were in it. In this dream you said this: *Would you rather be rich, envied and loathed as a fake – or poor, happy and respected for who you really are?*'

'I said that in your dream?'

'Yes, you did, and it was your best ever question. You were right to ask it.'

'How can I be right when this was just a dream and I never said it? And by the way, I don't ask closed, rhetorical and loaded questions.'

Dexter brushed this protest aside as a feeble irrelevance. 'No, you were right. I've decided. I'm not doing that phoney life any more.'

In an earlier book I wrote a chapter about questioning as a coaching technique, calling it 'Simple but not Easy: The Skilled Language of Coaching'. I made the point that the best coaching questions are deceptively simple: short and pithy. They are open, they give no hint about the questioner's point of view. It was a first for me to have a question attributed to me that I had never asked, to have it breach all my own principles of what constitutes a good coaching question and then to have it pronounced my best question.

Dexter did say no to the reality show. His celeb life trickled quietly to a close, along with his marriage.

In due course he enrolled under his real name for a music degree and was only rarely identified as the former celebrity, Dexter; and if he was, it was of little interest to fellow students twenty-five years younger.

At that point I lost touch with him.

I am not a believer in the predictive power of dreams, but I do believe they often uncover our most discomfiting dilemmas.

Several years after working with Dexter, my husband had just died and I was struggling to come to terms with my sorrow and anger: how dared he leave me to face old age alone? I was struggling with my guilt: I could have done so much more for him. I was struggling with my pain at his suffering, so uncomplainingly borne through a lifetime of steadily increasing disability. I was struggling with my worries at the cost, both actual and psychological, of providing care for him. I was struggling with missing him all day, every day: who would ever understand me, put up with me or be as unequivocally on my side as he was? Even after one of our most petty and shaming bickerings, there was never any doubt about our commitment to one another.

Was there ever a clearer case for projecting on to others what we cannot bear in ourselves? I talked often about how I loathed self-pity, yet here I was indulging in it daily.

Then one night I had a vivid dream. In my dream, Alan appeared to me, smiling jovially as he had so often done in life with his uncrackable good humour. 'My death was all a joke! Just a bit of fun!' And here he used his private pet name for me which I cannot write here. 'I'm not dead! See, I'm alive and I'm cured!'

I woke feeling joy which quickly turned to the crushing disappointment of realizing that my dream had merely and ruthlessly revealed my choices – which were exactly what they had been the night before. I could give way to self-pity, looking to my adult sons as a way of getting my narcissistic needs met: to be looked after, trying to make them – suffering equally with grievous loss – responsible for my happiness. I think of this as the Queen Victoria Option, a woman whose adored husband died young and who then spent many of her remaining forty years in relentless mourning, experiencing what we would now call *complicated grief*. Or I could step into the perilous abyss of living alone for the first time in my life, going on learning and developing, ignoring the puzzled voices of certain friends who constantly asked me when I was going to 'retire' or who enquired whether I was 'still' working, implying there was something truly weird about someone working when they seemed not to need to do so for any reason that a sensible person could understand.

At about this time I read one of those 'Where are they now?' features where journalists track down formerly famous persons. There is often something sneering about these pieces. They can read as if the journalist is looking for misery and failure. Dexter was one of the interviewees.

He described himself as a happy man, doing a variety of free-lance projects which built on his musical expertise and living in a part of the UK far from London. One of the standard questions in the interview was about turning points in life. Dexter's reply was that he had worked with an (unnamed) coach who had asked him the question, 'Would you rather be rich, envied and loathed as a fake – or poor, happy and respected for who you really are?'

After reading this I tracked down Dexter's email address. I told him how delighted I was to hear of his contentment, congratulated him on his fulfilling work and happy life, including the new relationship reported in the piece, and reminded him that I had never actually asked the question he had quoted.

His reply: 'Oh, but you did, you did! And you were so right to ask it. It's the best question anyone has ever asked me in my entire life.'

The Cure for Chocolate

Nadine approached me after hearing me at a conference where I had talked briefly about coaching people who needed to lose weight.

She spoke so quietly that I had to ask her to repeat what she was saying. Despite her notable height she seemed to be sagging as she bent towards me. She pointed mournfully to her ample body and said, 'Will you help me? I can tell you now that I'm a binge eater and I don't know how to stop. Give me a packet of chocolate biscuits at midnight and by fifteen minutes past I'll have eaten the lot. Am I a lost cause do you think? Is there any hope for me? Is there a cure for chocolate?'

This development had found its way into my coaching portfolio because so many of my clients had disclosed discomfort with their weight. In their first session I routinely ask people about physical and mental health along with questions about friends and family, leisure, housing, financial security, partner and career. The answers to the questions about health had often led to discussions about exercise and eating, and sometimes to revelations about incipient metabolic disorders or arthritic conditions strongly linked with being overweight, all of them with the potential for interference with performance at work and happiness in general. I was sympathetic. At a challenging time in my own life I had gained far too many pounds. I was engaged in a project where I was away from home for weeks at a time, living in hotels with beautiful food. It was all too easy to find comfort in eating and in seeming not to notice how the pounds piled on. I had found that working with my own coach meant steadily losing the pounds and staying at a normal weight ever since.

My original weight-loss clients had described getting fatter than was comfortable through a gradual process of eating slightly too much over a long period of time, just as I had myself. There was no real pathology behind their weight problems. Once their motivation was established and we looked at their eating patterns, healthier options could be reinforced through coaching.

Nadine represented a type of client who was significantly different. These people were often more than double their ideal weight, with years of yo-yo dieting behind them. They reported the intense shame of being stigmatized for their size, sometimes feeling certain they had failed to get jobs because of their weight. They were insulted in the street, they had fellow passengers openly reproach them on buses. They were forced to ask for the seat-belt extension on planes. They struggled with the physical discomforts of chafing thighs and breathlessness. All knew that they should be taking exercise but were too embarrassed to use a swimming pool or go to a gym. Some were self-aware enough to realize that being obese is like wearing your misery on the outside and that this is potentially a source of additional patronizing pity.

Nadine had been born into a family where there was little money. Her father started his working life on building sites as a labourer, but then established his own successful carpentry firm.

'He'd had a difficult childhood himself and it was impossible to get any praise from him. His natural instinct was to shout and criticize, and there was quite a bit of slapping,' she said.

London is not really the anonymous city of legend. When, as I have, you have lived for a long time in one part of it, it comes to seem more like a series of urban villages with an intricate web of multiple connections through neighbours, work and family. Islington is typical of many London boroughs in this respect. It has politicians, writers, people celebrated for their work in the performing arts, thousands of people from a wide range of other countries as well as the many locals who have lived in it all their lives. We all rub along pretty well. Nadine and I discovered we were near neighbours and had a number of acquaintances and interests in common.

I did not use euphemisms with these clients by talking about being 'big', 'plus-size', 'heavyset' or 'having a few extra pounds'. We faced it together: they were fat. I asked Nadine to bring me a selection of photographs from as many different stages of her life as possible. 'I want you to tell me the history of the fat through the pictures,' I said.

The story began with a chubby toddler sitting in the sun, her mouth smeared with chocolate.

Nadine's mother was Italian. 'That's my mum's doing,' she said. 'When she and my dad had a row it was often over me, and she'd take me off secretly and give me chocolate, you know, that Italian Mama thing.'

This was the pattern: reproach, shouting, followed by the comforting sweetness of chocolate as consolation. Then there were some thinner years with clippings from newspapers as a local swimming champion. When she failed to make a national youth team, her father had expressed his disappointment through spiteful comment and harsh criticism. By sixteen she was once more overweight. A little later her graduation picture showed her staring at the camera, bigger still, blank-faced and puffy. But the most startling images were from her wedding. There she was: svelte, statuesque, her husband beside her.

'I know,' said Nadine sadly, 'you have to look more than twice to recognize that this was the same person. Look at me now.' I did look and it was hard to see the powerful young swimmer or the glowing bride in the woman in front of me. She looked defeated, slumped. Again, she spoke so softly that I often had to ask her to repeat what she had said.

Had Nadine been unlucky, or had she unerringly chosen to marry someone who was a bully, just like her father? Either way, she had chosen badly. It had begun well. Her husband had picked her out at a disco. Tom had told her he could reinvent her as a beauty, courted her with holidays, jewellery, flattery. The extra pounds disappeared.

'I couldn't believe my good fortune,' she said. 'He took me shopping, he knew what would suit me, he was like my personal stylist. I adored him, he was generous with his money, the sex was amazing. My parents thought he was God.'

As soon as they married, the physical violence and verbal cruelty started. It began with pushing her around impatiently and continued with hurtful comments about her appearance. At that stage her weight was completely normal for her height, but he told her she looked like a Russian weightlifter, or said, 'Look at your huge shoulders, you're like one of those man-women at the Olympics.' He told her she was 'loud' and should lower her voice. He prevented her from applying for a promotion at work and was violently critical if she gave even the smallest glance to another man. He kept her away from parties unless he was her close escort. He cut her off from her friends. He began referring to her as 'The Eyetie', intended as an insulting reference to her Italian mother, or telling her that she had a moustache (she didn't).

At the point where Nadine and I met she had separated legally from Tom after her latest bruises could not be explained away to an inquisitive brother. She had also gained many pounds in weight.

'How do you feel about living alone?' I asked.

'Terrible. I'm not designed for it. I need to have a man in my life. But who will even look at me when I look like I do? I couldn't undress in front of a new man – it would be too shaming.'

When you want to make any major change in your life it helps to have the frightening data about what will happen if you do nothing set side by side with the glorious gains of making the change. If the fear is overwhelming, we typically get paralysed by indecision. If the benefits are unclear, we may also dither. This is why I suggested that these clients booked a date with their GPs to get their blood lipids analysed, their blood pressure and blood sugar measured. Nadine was compliant, though she winced when I made my request. She had already been the recipient of many severe lectures from her doctor. This latest visit revealed borderline diabetes, dangerously high blood pressure, a Body Mass Index of 32 and worrying blood lipids results. 'Are you determined to die young?' she quoted him as saying. 'Because, if so, you're definitely on the right track.'

The central mystery of gaining so much weight is this: when people know that they are stigmatized, when they are humiliated daily, loathe their body shape as much as all of them do, when they know that the health risks include life-shortening illnesses, when their excessive weight threatens their relationships, when they tell you that they long to be thin, why do they go on eating in ways they know to be so unwise?

The dazzling pioneers of therapy such as Freud and Jung presented their cases as a kind of detective fiction where the superior intelligence of the therapist solves the whodunit of the client's wretchedness through applying apparently scientific labels, such as *neuroticism* or *oedipal complex*. In coaching, the philosophy is the opposite. Many clients expect advice, wisdom and interpretations from their coach, but as I explained to Nadine, the coach plays the role of Dr Watson, the plodding, loyal questioner, and the client plays Sherlock Holmes because the client is the one who knows all their secrets and is the world's leading expert on themselves.

Nadine and I explored the question of hidden pay-offs because there always is one when you fail to do what you say you want so badly. What does it do for a fat person to stay so fat? What's the perverse pay-off? Pursuing this line, I said to her, 'Okay, Sherlock, make the connection for me between Tom's abuse and getting fat. What was the hidden benefit?'

There was a long pause before the hesitant answer. 'He absolutely hated fat. Couldn't bear it. The more he criticized it, the fatter I got. I saw a therapist and she told me I did "emotional eating", which is right, I do, but that doesn't answer the question why, does it?'

We coaches all hope for *ah-ha* moments for our clients, especially if we have cunningly provided the clues ourselves. But there was no need for that here.

'I think,' said Nadine slowly, 'that it was maybe my one way of getting back at him though I wasn't aware of it at the time. And it kept him away sexually because when we did have sex it was always rough sex and he told me it was "like poking a lard bucket" and he was only doing it because it was good for me. Could there be anything more humiliating?'

It is easy to believe that insight on its own is enough to change behaviour, but my experience is that it is not. Although she was legally separated from him, Tom called her frequently. He sent gifts, suggested meals, treats, a drink. Nadine was always tempted to agree and sometimes she replied to his texts. Sometimes she met him.

Telling me about this at a subsequent session, she said, 'The trouble is, I still love him.'

'What do you love, exactly?' I asked, reminding her of the appalling behaviour he had perpetrated on her.

Nadine could not answer at first. Then she said, 'I suppose it's the idea of him, the person I thought I was marrying all that time ago. But that's not really him, is it?'

While these conversations were continuing, we were also discussing food. We started with eating a meal together where I asked Nadine to tell me her thoughts and feelings.

'Embarrassment – I want to gulp it all down, but I'm aware you're eating a lot more slowly.'

'So how rapidly do you normally eat?'

'Very rapidly. I think I hardly notice the food. My focus is on how much I want to fill the hunger.'

I asked, 'What are you hungry for?'

The answer came quickly. 'Love. But I'm afraid of love and I'm afraid of food.'

'You're afraid of love and afraid of food. What are these fears about for you?'

'That I'm nothing, that I don't matter, that I'm invisible.'

Food is an inert substance. It cannot fill an emotional vacuum, but Nadine had learnt very early in life that it might. She had fetishized food, and the more she saw it as 'dangerous' the more attractive it became and the less pleasant it was to eat. It is a paradox of being overweight that you cannot enjoy what you are eating. Bingeing is quickly followed by shame and self-loathing.

I gave Nadine a handsome notebook and asked her to keep a journal, logging her relationships with food, noting her mood before, during and after eating. At this stage, apart from suggesting the food diary, we had done nothing that would be standard in almost all approaches to weight loss. These usually start with getting weighed and then setting targets for losing weight. Throughout the entire time we worked together I never knew what Nadine's starting weight had been and we never set a single target.

At our seventh meeting Nadine announced that she had reached a turning point. 'I've decided to go for divorce,' she said. 'I don't want him in my life any more.'

Several weeks passed. At our next session Nadine strode into the room looking exhilarated. 'Look!' she said, waggling the front of her jacket to create a billowing space, the same jacket she had been wearing when we first met. It now looked many sizes too big. 'I've worn it specially to show you. You could get a litter of puppies into the gap!' It was true. Her symbol of success was that she was now able to shop at Marks & Spencer instead of having to buy clothing from what she called 'Fat Lady Brands' on the internet where no one could comment on her size.

The people around us often have every reason to keep us stuck exactly as we are. Hearing about the detail of a coaching session will sometimes encourage scoffing and undermining. This is especially true where other people in the client's life have gained psychological advantage from their supposed moral superiority, for instance being thin where the other person is fat. For this reason, I usually counsel clients not to say too much about their sessions to their closest friends and family. But where clients are enthused and motivated, they may well ignore such advice. Nadine was alight with energy about her steady weight loss. She was going to tell everyone, and she insisted that this had to include Tom. She had realized that she no longer needed the defence of overeating. There really was a cure for chocolate.

A few weeks later I was having a quiet supper at home with my sons. They live locally, we are close, and they often drop in for an impromptu meal. The buzzer at the outer entrance to my flat sounded. I looked up in puzzlement. 'Who's that? I'm not expecting anyone.' I live in a gated building with a concierge and the kind of entry system that discourages cold callers. The picture on the video was fuzzy and a voice I didn't recognize said, 'Delivery.'

I opened my front door as the lift arrived. A young man emerged holding something that could have been a pizza delivery bag.

'I've come from Tom –,' he said, naming Nadine's husband, scowling fiercely. 'Tom's a good friend of Mr –, know who I mean?' There was a pause here for extra menace to make sure I knew he was referring to our most notorious local felon, a man whose name is widely known in Islington. 'Tom says you're to stop interfering with his domestic stuff – or else. You won't like what would happen. Know what I mean?'

My sons emerged from behind me. They are both over six feet tall. My visitor was noticeably smaller and possibly slightly puny-looking. He looked alarmed, his little bit of swagger gone in a moment.

'Hey, it's Lego Man!' said one son, quickly stepping forward and initiating a high-five greeting. 'How are you, mate? What are you up to these days?'

'Oh yeah, man!' said the other son, fluent as ever in London-speak. 'What brings you to Mum's gaff?'

Alas for the would-be hard man, sent allegedly and utterly improbably by the notorious Mr – on behalf of Nadine's husband. My sons had instantly recognized him as one of the group of kids who had 'played out' amicably and for many years in the unusually safe and traffic-free street where they had all grown up. This street is typical of Islington, where social housing is inextricably mixed with privately owned properties. There were many families in that street who struggled to keep going. There were single mothers who had to blend poorly paid work with doing their best for their children. There were other families whose lives had been blighted by bereavement, prison sentences, disability or unemployment. Yet inhabitants of the street also included a celebrity newsreader and a member of the House of Lords. These social differences seemed to be invisible to the children, perhaps because they all went to the same schools.

I now recognized our visitor myself as Keith, a shy little boy nicknamed Lego Man because of his excessive love for this product, one of a large family who had many times visited our then house. His face was an instant scarlet; he muttered something which may have been an apology and fled towards the lift, which fortunately for him was still waiting at my floor. As he left, I called after him, 'Keith, you will tell Tom – not to bother me in future, won't you?' My door gave a crisp little slam as we shut it. My sons and I looked at each other for a moment and then fell into snorts of giggling.

I did not tell Nadine about this visit.

Nadine and I had a few more sessions. We talked about her divorce and how to minimize the temporary anguish it might cause. We talked about managing dietary lapses and how to get back on track. We talked about her new life as a single woman and what this would mean in terms of how she presented herself to the world. We talked about how to get around her fear that her steady weight loss was just a temporary blip.

Nadine's divorce went through with minimal hassle. Her health improved dramatically. She changed her phone number. Her former husband moved his business out of London and disappeared from her life. Her parents died and left her a useful legacy. She changed jobs, more than doubled her previous salary, moved house, has married again and has a child. She still lives in Islington.

As for me, the appeal of other specialist aspects of coaching replaced my interest in weight loss and I closed down that strand of my work.

I occasionally see Nadine in our busy local street market. Just recently, encountering her this way, I suggested that we gave ourselves the treat of a cup of coffee at a little cafe in the middle of the market. In the summer you can sit outside and watch the world go by. She gave me her card.

'You've changed your name!'

'Yes. I'm calling myself Nadia and I'm using an Italian surname, my mum's maiden name. I'm so proud of my Italian heritage. Islington is special because of the Italian community that settled here in the nineteenth century. Being bilingual has helped me at work, I'm using my languages constantly – I've learnt German too and I'm pretty fluent.'

It was a hot day and she was wearing a sleeveless T-shirt. She caught me glancing at her formidable shoulders. 'Yes, I've got my swimmer's shoulders back,' she laughed. 'And I'm doing volunteer coaching for nervous non-swimmers who'd like to learn. It's great fun.' I noticed her strong voice and the directness of her smile. This tall, confident woman had little resemblance to the stooped, overweight ghost whom I had met at that conference.

Getting thin was never what her coaching had been about; instead it had been about permission to be herself.

I thought it was time to tell her about my visitor. She was appalled, alarmed and ready to feel guilty.

'Don't worry about it,' I said. I pointed to a stall in the market. 'I occasionally used to see Keith serving there and he always blushed when he saw me, but maybe his career as incompetent menacer caught up with him because he hasn't been there for some time.'

I was silent for a moment as I remembered the boys from our street. One of that little gang had enrolled at the Anna Scher Children's Theatre just around the corner and went on to become a famous TV soap actor. Against all the odds of overcoming disadvantage in childhood, another has become a senior civil servant while his brother is a teacher; one is a successful plumber whose vans I spot everywhere. I see some of the others out and about with their wives and children.

But Keith? Somehow I thought that life might not have been so kind to him.

Witness

It can be tempting as a coach to think that you know all about a client. Many years as a coach have taught me that even when a client is palpably open, making themselves vulnerable in a way they are unlikely to do with many other people, what they hold back can be the most important thing.

On a mild early autumn day, Jamie and I were walking along the towpath of the Regent's Canal in London. It was cool enough to justify a jacket but not chilly enough for gloves. Yet Jamie had his hands jammed into the pockets of his coat. It was windless and sunny, but his shoulders were hunched as if against some wintry breeze that only he could feel.

'I know I'm in trouble,' he said, 'but what am I to do? I really can't seem to help it.'

We were walking instead of sitting inside a warm coaching room because Jamie was a self-confessed fidget. I had seen it for myself in our first session when he had waggled his long, lean legs, drummed his thighs with his hands and continually twisted in his chair. Was it the quality of my seating, or was it something else, I had asked.

'I'm restless anyway, but for someone with a reputation for fierceness, I'm feeling nervous.'

'What's that about, can you tell me?'

'I'm one of those bad boys. I feel I've been sent to the head-mistress.'

It was true that Jamie had been 'sent'. In the sharp competition for talent in media circles, often written and reverently referred to by media insiders as 'The Talent', bad-boy behaviour can be tolerated for much longer than would be considered sensible elsewhere.

Jamie's gift was for directing rather than performing. A shrewd production company creates close relationships with the producers and directors who will bring style, flair, kudos – and investment – to a high-profile project, knowing that in this largely freelance world, loyalty is fragile. More recently even than at the time when this work with Jamie took place, you can still see the reluctance of media executives to confront 'Talent' that misbehaves.

Although such tolerance is rarer on the other side of the stage or camera, there are many directors whose obsessive perfectionism has drifted into bullying. So there is the film director who allegedly keeps a nail gun for handily nailing mobile phones to the wall if the crew's devices go off at inappropriate moments, the one who arranged for real cadavers to be produced on set to obtain more convincing expressions of horror from actors and very many who have goaded and pestered their performers so that they produce real rather than confected crying. More recently, when Harvey Weinstein's career as a Hollywood producer suddenly unravelled, it set off an unstoppable domino effect of revelations involving the inappropriate use of status, of widespread sexual harassment in theatre, music, politics and many other spheres. It became clear how invulnerable and powerful such men had felt for so long.

Jamie's problems were nothing like so serious and there was never the slightest hint of sexual misconduct. But he was in trouble and not for the first time. There had been a number of incidents where he had upset crew members and production staff.

One such exchange was faithfully captured on a bystander's phone. When uploaded on to Twitter, many people quickly added sharp comments of their own and then it was no longer possible for Jamie to defend his words as harmless banter nor for his employers to pretend that his behaviour did not matter.

It is unusual for an organization to commission coaching for a freelancer. Probably it only happened here because the distinguished executive in charge had himself benefited from coaching, understood its potential to produce change and saw in Jamie someone who could bring long-term benefit to the company. It was generous but it was also a canny commercial decision. When calling to discuss the assignment, this man had said, 'I'm contacting you because I hear you have a reputation for being direct. But I warn you now that he will probably try one of his charm offensives and he may play games.'

'How might he play games?'

'He hasn't worked with actors without learning a thing or two. He might pretend to be coached while laughing up his sleeve and telling his mates that it was all a waste of time.'

'Nothing is more obvious to a coach than a client who is just pretending,' I said. 'But I'll be able to judge when I sound him out. If I have any concerns, I'll raise them, and if those concerns won't go away, I'll say no, just as he will be able to raise any concerns he has about me and to decide whether I'm the right coach for him.'

Any doubts in my own mind disappeared in that first phone call. Jamie was humble, interested and open. 'This is potentially crushing for me,' he said, 'and I have to find ways of managing it.'

I had avoided saying to Jamie's sponsor that I often turn down such assignments. People who cannot manage their anger can make for resentful clients. They will tell me that the problems lie with the pesky incompetence and deliberately infuriating habits of others. These annoying others *made* them lash out, they provoked it, it was their own fault if they felt the sharp edge of a cleverer person's tongue. For goodness' sake, what does anyone expect? The patience of a saint? Life's too short, bosses should not employ idiots.

Jamie did have one version of this familiar script. He believed his outbursts happened as mysterious eruptions that were beyond his control. At the same time, he acknowledged that getting a reputation as a director who gave way to tantrums, especially when you were still building your reputation, was likely to be career derailment in waiting.

'I guess this will sound pretentious,' he said, 'but I want to write and direct my own features, I want to be that poncy thing, an auteur!' He wanted to bring his passion for storytelling to the big screen or maybe to streaming services like Netflix, Hulu or Amazon, where sizeable budgets could be available. All of this was unlikely to happen in the current climate if, despite his evident talent, there were question marks around his ability to manage himself, question marks that raised the possibility of future scandal, frightening studios and investors away.

Our sessions began. They invariably started with at least five minutes of scurrilous and very funny gossip told with elan. There was this famous actor who got out-of-control drunk at the Toronto Film Festival, that composer whose commission was cancelled because the score was so terrible, the TV star who looked likely to be outed at last as gay. Perhaps this was the charm offensive that his boss had mentioned. If so, I'm afraid that I fell for it. Along with this, there were many references to his family where I had seen innumerable photographs on his phone: his wife and the three little boys, the last one of whom was, he said, 'Our amazing surprise. We thought we'd stopped, but then this young ruffian, Angus, came along.' When he mentioned his wife, his voice softened. 'She's given me the family I never really had. My childhood was pretty miserable.'

It was no surprise to hear that there was a difficult family background. Thanks to urging from his wife, Jamie had found a therapist at a famous London clinic.

'I learnt that it was classic stuff. The overbearing father who blamed me for being born and somehow killing my mother. She died because of a complication from giving birth to me. Then the second wife. Poor old thing. She was the nurse at the school where my father taught, same school I went to, and she was in her late thirties, on her last chance to get a husband and a child. Puppy-dog personality – she needed a man. My father was desperate for a nanny and housekeeper who would share his bed, so she landed him. She was useless against my dad's temper, just fluttering about sobbing in the background. Her kids, my half-sisters, retreated into those roles you can read about if you google "dysfunctional family". The older one just hid and read Enid Blyton all day long, the younger one was Daddy's little princess and her role was to simper or be the clown.'

There was no disguising the cold sarcasm in this account. I had already guessed the answer to my question, 'And you? What role did you play?'

'I was the scapegoat, the conduit for all that was wrong in that family, the one who answered back, who refused to call his wife "Mummy" and called her by her name, Sheila, instead. I was the one who got the slipper on my bum or my legs and was told I was insolent. Then because he always whacked me too hard and got frightened he'd overdone it, he'd creep up to my bedroom and say sorry and promise that it was the last time, but it never was.'

When Jamie was fourteen, one of the school's sports coaches overheard other boys joking in the shower about Jamie's bruises. Jamie was questioned. The school was a little ahead of its time and had at least some child safeguarding policies in place. Jamie's father was still teaching at the school. The headmaster had 'a quiet word' with him and that was the end of the beatings, though not of the verbal abuse that had gone with them.

This was the story Jamie told me as we walked the towpath on that autumn day. He said he knew the therapy had been valuable because it had shown him that his family was not unique. It had answered the question 'Why?' as in 'Why do I behave the way I do?' But the therapy had been brief, just four sessions. It had not answered the question 'What?' as in 'What should I do about the anger?'

I told Jamie that I thought he still had some preparatory work to do. This was to understand fully the impact of his behaviour, positive and negative, on the people around him. Mostly we do not truly understand this: we have heard the hints, we may even know the headlines, but we will typically underplay how much any of it matters.

'You started your career as a journalist. If you were to take yourself as your own investigative project, how would you approach it?'

'Ha! Leave that thought with me!'

Three weeks later a video arrived in my inbox. The only words in the email were, 'Puma or Pussycat? See link.'

Now we were back on the canal towpath. It was November, the air felt raw, there was some faint mist clinging to the water and gloves were definitely needed. When you are walking rather than sitting you do not have that relentless eye contact with the other person. Sometimes it is easier to say and hear difficult things. We ended up sitting side by side on a bench next to what had been a lock-keeper's cottage and were each nursing a take-away coffee cup from one of the many cafes in Broadway Market. The discussion lasted a lot longer than it took to sip the coffee. We both had iPads open and referred to Jamie's video frequently.

Jamie had done what he described as 'Vox pop by ambush'. He had asked innumerable people – supporters and known critics alike, seniors, juniors, crew, actors – for their unguarded impressions of him, whipping out his phone to record their replies. His only question had been, 'What's it like working with me?' The messages of the video were clear. People loved Jamie's humour, his extravagant enthusiasm, his inventiveness with sound and vision, his concern for quality, his gift for casting, his idealistic ambition for whatever the project was. At the same time, they dreaded the sudden rages which came and went so unpredictably. Many declared their fear of him.

Jamie said he was mortified. 'These little wobblies are over in a trice for me,' he said. 'I forget all about whatever's provoked it.'

'But it's not over for them in a trice and they don't forget,' I said. 'They don't see them as amusing eccentricities or *wobblies*. Your explosions make them wary. They don't trust you to be calm. If they're afraid, they're likely to underperform. As you can see from your video, what you believe is light humour where you think of yourself as the target, they see as withering put-downs aimed at them. It means you're not getting the best out of people. Only the bravest will answer back because of your powerful position.'

It was no surprise to hear Jamie mutter, 'But I don't feel powerful, that's just the point.' As he said this, I noticed that his restlessness seemed to have gone away. He sat quietly, hands in his lap.

We had been there for about an hour. It had become chillier and I noticed we had been joined by one of the many birds that live on the canal, a handsome coot that had flapped out of the water and then, on spindly yellow legs, delicately picked its way to us and stood calmly, its sharp white beak just inches from our feet, for the last minutes of our conversation.

The light was fading as the afternoon dwindled into dusk. As we left, the coot strode away then pattered noisily over the water before taking off.

There is no mystery about how to master unproductive anger. Everything depends on motivation. Even the most habitually aggressive person can learn better control over their impulsive eruptions if they understand how much is at stake, especially if they can confront their excuses. Jamie did. Over several further sessions we looked at some classic anger-management techniques. These involve separating the trigger from the response and understanding that you have a choice about what you do, even if the choice lasts microseconds. This is a challenge to people who believe that their habitual reactions are out of their control. You do this by recognizing then anticipating the typical situations which provide the trigger. Many of the most success-ful techniques then involve the age-old advice about counting to ten before replying. Jamie also learnt how to use 'I statements' rather than 'you statements', such as 'I am feeling annoyed' rather than 'you are annoying', and to frame his responses as a future-focused problem that needs both parties to find a solution rather than as a past-focused problem that is all about what the other person has allegedly done wrong.

Jamie had had no more violent outbursts and was cautiously optimistic about his ability to change for good. Just before what would have been our final session I had a brief email: 'My father has died suddenly. He had a massive stroke. Sheila is in hysterics and my sisters are useless. I'm needed to sort out the funeral etc. I'll be in touch.'

Jamie's father had moved out of schoolteaching and into a senior administrative role. Jamie sent me links to a few bland obituaries describing his father's career and the short-lived re-tirement that had followed it. I noticed that his name had been James and that he had been the son of another James.

The winter passed. Every now and then I would get an email saying, 'Hope you're well. I haven't forgotten there's more to do, just keeping in touch, I'll be back.'

Then he was. 'Everything has calmed down now,' said the email. 'Let's meet in the usual place on the canal. Lots to discuss.'

I walked the short distance from my apartment to the bench on the canal towpath overlooking the City Basin where Jamie and I had agreed to meet. He stood up to greet me, enjoying my surprise.

'I'm on childcare duty today because there's no nursery – and it's my turn. This is Gus,' he said, pointing to the small boy lolling in a buggy. 'Say hello to Jenny, Gus.' Gus gave a three-year-old's wriggle of shyness, then a big smile, gravely holding out a small paw for me to shake. Jamie said, 'Let's head off to Broadway Market as usual and we can buy Gus a bun.'

While we walked, I asked about the impact of his father's death. Jamie said it had been a shock because it was unexpected, but he had been unable to feel grief.

'As a child, I desperately wanted his love and admiration, but that intervention from the school made me see him in a different light and I came to despise him for his cowardice and aggression. Sheila accused me of being cruel to deprive him of his grandchildren, but I knew it was better to reduce contact to a minimum. I rarely saw him or my sisters after I left for university. My wife's family have more than made up for what I missed. They're warm, welcoming and accepting.'

At the funeral, Jamie said that his aunt, his father's sister, had talked for the first time about her guilt, knowing of the beatings and not intervening.

'Shame prevented it, social shame, the need to keep up appearances and all that bollocks. It was annoying to hear this kind of justification, but I stayed calm. She also told me what I already knew, that Grandad James had beaten my father and that his father had done the same. She seemed to think that excused it.'

Now we were at the cafe and instead of carrying out the drinks we were sitting inside. We had some lively conversation with Gus who struck me as unusually articulate and spirited for a three-and-a-half-year-old. He told me how he loved painting and drawing at nursery, about his best friends – a real one called Joshua and an imaginary one called Big Penfold – and about his older brothers. He seemed a happy, smiley child.

We ordered scones and tea, juice for Gus. The scones were not fresh. The texture was gritty, the butter tasted rancid.

Gus took one bite and spat it out. 'Yuk!' he said, in a voice loud enough to draw frowns from people at the other tables. 'This is yuk. I want ice cream!'

'Gus,' said Jamie quietly. 'That is not acceptable. If you don't like food, you don't spit it out and you don't say yuk. It's rude to the people in the cafe and it's embarrassing for Jenny and me to see you do that. You're not having ice cream. I'd like you to say sorry.'

Gus bellowed and screamed. His face flamed purple, his eyes bulged, he hurled himself about in his seat. The people at the next table stared and clucked their disapproval.

'Gus,' said Jamie. His voice was quiet and firm. 'I'm telling you again, you're not going to get ice cream and you are going to stop shouting.'

Jamie looked at me calmly. 'We ignore this. He'll run out of steam soon.' The roaring stopped and subsided into tragedian's gulps. Jamie leant towards his little son. 'And I think you have something to say?'

Gus bridled then mumbled, 'Sorry!'

'Good boy, you did that nicely, now we can forget all about it. You see, Gus, you'll find that by shouting less you will be heard more.' Jamie winked and shot me a glance while he said this. *Shouting less in order to be heard more* had been one of the mantras I had suggested to him. He ruffled Gus's hair.

While Jamie was paying the bill, Gus tugged on my hand. He looked up at me and in a clear, confident voice, loud enough to be heard by most of the people at nearby tables, declared, 'I'm never coming here again!'

I suppressed a smile. I leant down and whispered, 'I agree. Me neither.'

Outside we sat on the same bench by the lock-keeper's cottage. Gus was back in his buggy, snuggled drowsily in a blanket. Jamie said, 'Through all of this, what I have never said to you is my dread that my father's pattern and his father's pattern, and back probably through the generations, would inevitably repeat itself in me and then in my own children. It's one of the reasons I decided to call myself Jamie not James. The therapist I saw unwittingly planted this idea in me by constantly talking about "transgenerational transmission of abuse". It was very depressing to hear, and she kept on and on about forgiving my father and that's why I stopped going to her. I can't forgive him and I've absolutely no regrets about that. It's been healthy to cut myself away from him. But I do know this cycle of abusive behaviour perpetuates itself that way. What you experience yourself can be what you visit on your children because it's what you know.'

The theme in all of this coaching had been a continued discussion about power and leadership. We had discussed how, underneath their bluster and apparent fearlessness, people who readily vent their anger or bully others are afraid. Often their fear is buried too deeply for them to access it, but it is there nonetheless. They fear losing face, they fear looking inadequate, they fear being exposed. They fear that others may be cleverer or more powerful, so they strike first. When you do this, you destroy trust, the foundation of any worthwhile relationship.

Jamie's fear was of being incompetent; we had had many hours discussing how achievement rather than power was what motivated him; that his need for competence had been overwhelming and handicapping. Everything he did was about quality and about his itch to improve things, to get faultless performance, especially from himself. Learning where good-enough would be enough and where perfection was essential was a distinction that he was realizing was possible. Moral authority is the only kind that really gives you power. You gain that through living the values that demonstrate liking and respect for other people.

As we sat in the weak spring sunshine, a coot once more appeared. This time six downy grey chicks were following. The parent bird came towards us and the chicks waddled behind, squeaking. 'Did you know they co-parent?' said Jamie. 'This little bird trusts us enough to come really close and with its precious chicks, it's amazing.'

Yet again that afternoon, we compared Jamie's motivation with the likely motivation of his father.

'His was purely about control and power for its own sake. He was a weak man. He needed to feel that he was in charge, whatever the situation. No wonder he was drawn to working in traditional schools where there was a rigid hierarchy. What you just saw in that cafe would have been enough to send my father into a cold fury. He might not have hit me there and then, but I would have been battered mercilessly later, that's for sure.'

'Yes,' I said, 'you are different. You are not your father.'

'The thing is, Jenny,' he said, 'I really have broken free, but I need you to be my witness. I never have and I never will hit or humiliate my sons. Will you do that? Will you be my witness?'

'Yes,' I said. 'I will be your witness.'

Little Miss Mouse

The time is long ago and I am in my boss's office at the BBC. He is a shy, somewhat donnish character who has worked his way up the ranks from having been a producer himself. A summons to his office is a rare event and I see at once that I am right to be nervous. He is normally a mild-mannered chap, but he looks furious. It turns out that I have made a grave error. I have put a well-known actor into one of my programmes *on the night that the same actor is in another programme made by a much more important department.* My boss has just returned from a ritual drubbing at the hands of his colleagues at the BBC's Television Programme Review Board, a weekly event where all new output is subjected to supposedly neutral and exquisitely judged comment from your peers. What had happened was what often took place, savage wit at other people's expense, especially if their departments were somewhere lower down the pecking order. He had been publicly slapped down for having allowed this appalling oversight to occur.

I can see myself now, speechless and blushing.

'But I had no idea that there was anything wrong in this . . . And I didn't know he [the actor] was in this other show . . . How could I have known?'

The tersely given answer was that I should have known. But I didn't. My boss gave no quarter. He was cold and angry. I had made a bad mistake, had let him and the department down, he expected better.

Poor boss. I see now that he was only doing to me what he had experienced himself – an unexpected kicking from more powerful people – and that he would have been told exactly what he was telling me: that he should somehow have known about and prevented this dreadful debacle.

Even now, decades later, my memory of the perceived unfairness and absurdity of the whole conversation has the power to spark indignation. How could I have known about a 'rule' that was never written down anywhere, especially when I rarely worked with actors as we were a department almost entirely devoted to making factual programmes? Was the television audience so dim that they did not understand what actors do? Surely the conversation could have been handled more skilfully? And wasn't it all a bit overblown when, as I and my colleagues so frequently said to each other, 'It's only television' – something that no one really believed as we all took ourselves and our programmes so extremely seriously.

After I crept away from his office I rejected everything he'd said. He was just wrong, it was unfair. In fact, if I could have delivered some unspeakable and unpunished revenge on him, I might have enjoyed doing it.

What would that boss say, I wonder, if I could remind him now about that conversation? It would probably be that all he was doing was his duty: he was giving me feedback.

We forget that the profession of manager is relatively young because it was unnecessary before people were clustered into factories and assumed to be too stupid to make decisions for themselves. There is only one reason for being a manager and that is to manage the performance of others. Everything else is just decoration, whether you are talking about how to inspire them through the splendour of your rhetoric, or about how smoothly ambassadorial you are with those more senior people inside and outside the organization, or about your admirable facility with budgets. All of this is secondary to being able to manage the performance of your staff. This means praising them when they get something right and telling them not to do it again when they get something wrong.

'Managing performance' is another bit of management jargon. In some organizations such as the NHS, it has turned itself into a verb – to performance manage. When used this way and in the passive tense it has sinister significance. If you are being *performance managed* it means you have finally captured the attention of your bosses, but not in a good way. You are most probably on your way out, where you become an embarrassment, someone to avoid. Everyone is afraid that some of your contagion will stick to them.

On more or less any standard management course there will be a session on how to give feedback. I have run many such sessions myself. Yet literally every month I work with coaching clients whose problem is that they cannot or will not give feedback.

Rachel was one such client. She was in her first senior managerial role. The HR director who made the original contact said, 'She's a lovely girl, but, well, not very firm.'

I privately noted the use of the word 'girl' to describe an adult woman, but merely asked, 'Not very firm? What does that mean in practice?'

'Er, well, her team kind of run rings around her, you know?'

'No, not really. Can you be a bit more specific?'

'Well, if she has someone in her team who hasn't delivered what they promised, she'll either ignore it, or say it doesn't matter, or redo it herself. If she carries on like this, she'll either burn herself out, or get moved sideways. Her boss is one of our most influential directors and he's told her she needs to harden up – we're in a highly competitive business. She doesn't seem to take it in. We see her as having promise because she's such a lovely person and so brilliant in so many ways, but she'll never be promoted if she can't crack it.'

There was a pause and then, 'Maybe I shouldn't tell you this, but her boss's nickname for her is Little Miss Mouse and that says it all really. Don't tell her that, will you?'

This unwillingness to give feedback is endemic in organizations. Did my HR contact see that in refusing to give Rachel direct feedback herself, she was faithfully repeating the pattern of which Rachel herself was accused? Probably not. The word feedback itself is often a misnomer. What I received from my boss all those years ago was not feedback but criticism and its purpose was to unload his humiliation on to me. When this is what happens the process will rarely if ever improve performance. Any sensible message buried inside it will be rejected by the receiver, who will probably merely become more adept at evading detection next time.

The first rule of giving genuine feedback is that you do it when you are unruffled enough to be direct but friendly. Its purpose is to benefit and develop the receiver. True feedback is a gift and there is a case for saying that withholding it is punitive. Yet it is rare for managers to learn what good practice looks like because giving feedback is usually done so badly. This probably explains why so many managers avoid doing it at all. Or, as in Rachel's case, ask a coach to do it instead.

At our first session Rachel greeted me enthusiastically with a firm handshake and a strong voice. She was notably warm in her manner. Unasked, she had brought me a cappuccino from the local Italian deli.

'I took a risk and thought, *I want some coffee myself, I think Jenny might like one too*, but in case you don't like cappuccino, I got a black one as well.'

Cappuccino is my tipple, so I was grateful for such a generous gesture at the same time as noticing how unusual it was.

I asked her what her own understanding was of why coaching had been suggested for her.

'They think I should be what they call tough.'

'And do you agree?'

'Not sure. I can't stand bullying and I see a lot of that around me, and I don't want to copy that example, but I suppose they might have a bit of a point.'

I asked Rachel what she wanted to get out of our work. The answer was that she wanted to be more comfortable in her role. And what would 'more comfortable' mean?

'I'd be working fewer hours and not working every weekend, for a start, and feeling less stressed and less put-upon. And I wouldn't have to listen to my boss telling me to toughen up, whatever that means.'

Rachel believed it was wrong for her not to do exactly the same tasks as everyone else; that where people struggled, it was your role as a boss to help them out. She thought that praise worked far better than punishment or criticism and that team harmony was the only way to get results. If putting harmony first and at all costs shades into rescuing and doing other people's work as well as your own it can be a sure way to exactly the situation that Rachel seemed to be in: overwork. At the same time, she was explicit in saying that she disliked the coercive climate she saw around her.

In that first session I asked Rachel to tell me about her childhood. Rachel hesitated. 'Oh, it was just dull really, a bit too much church and so on – maybe I'll tell you more when we know each other better.' I had to be content with that for the time being.

At a later session we discussed what 'tough' might mean. I asked Rachel for examples of times when in her own view she had been what she would define as 'tough'. There was a pause before she said, 'I think it's time to tell you my story.'

Rachel was born into a family that was part of a fundamentalist Christian group. They were a tiny splinter group, but like the parent sect, they excluded anyone who was not part of the 'Brotherhood'. Family groups employed each other, the Brotherhood ran their own small schools for the youngest children and enforced strict behavioural rules. There was no television, no radio, no cinema, no theatre, no dancing. Women and girls had to be subservient to men, and women were made responsible for the sexual conduct of men. As a girl or woman you could not go outside with your head uncovered. Clothing was drab and make-up was forbidden. If you persistently defied these rulings, you would be punished. This included being subjected to a process called 'shutting up', where you were imprisoned in your own home.

Rachel explained that any former member of this sect would know, as she did, about 'the Three Fs' associated with trying to leave. These were: Fear – of eternal damnation; Finance – having no money or means of support; Family – being forbidden any contact because if you were excommunicated you were treated as dead and no further contact was allowed.

Rachel's sect was too small and too geographically isolated to run secondary schools. In a mainstream school at eleven years old, she defied imprecations about remaining separate and quietly made several friends. Her parents had insisted she should be withdrawn from Religious Studies classes but from the age of fourteen she had somehow managed to attend them. Aged fifteen, she had publicly challenged the literal truth of the Bible during a service. She said she believed that it was a book with human origins based on an oral tradition, taking its place among several other such texts like the Torah and the Qur'an. Her punishment was two weeks of 'shutting up'. When she remained defiantly unrepentant, she had several beatings from both parents for shaming the family. Two days after her sixteenth birthday, Rachel crept out of her home in the middle of the night and took refuge with the parents of her closest school friend. Despite threats of court action, this was where she remained until she went to university. Over the years she had managed to have three clandestine meetings with her sister but no other contact with the rest of her family.

'So you see, that's why I know about bullying.'

Rachel began asking colleagues for feedback. She learnt that people appreciated her kindness, her ability to read people sensitively, her professional expertise, her generosity. They also wanted her to delegate more, to be clearer about standards, more straightforward in saying what she wanted, and to be more direct in her own feedback. One person had been brave enough to tell her that her boss referred to her as 'Little Miss Mouse'. Far from being shocked at this news, Rachel was thoughtful. 'Mice are persistent, aren't they, and it's harder to get rid of them than people think.'

Rachel was an assiduous client. We practised the apparently simple protocol for giving people feedback where you start with a calm statement by using the words 'I noticed' or 'I observed', followed by a factual description of specific behaviour. Then you describe the impact on you. Then you ask the person to behave differently, pause to get their views and agree what to do in the future. This avoids all the usual feedback traps of dumping anger on the recipient, generalizing by using phrases such as 'you always', or making wholesale criticisms of the person's character. We also practised making requests and learning how to say no, something that involves putting your own needs first.

Shortly after this, Rachel arrived for her session, face alight, saying she had something to tell me that she thought might intrigue me. 'It's that feedback thing in action,' she said.

At a routine meeting, her boss had been well launched into what Rachel described as 'one of his regular random tirades where we all get a tongue-lashing'. She had waited for a pause and had then challenged his interpretation of events with some solid evidence. He had whipped round and left his seat, advancing on her. He was a bulky man; he had put his face inches away from hers.

'He was close enough for me to smell his meaty sweat,' she said. He had hissed, 'I run this operation, okay, Little Miss Mouse?'

There had been an appalled silence in the room.

Rachel said, 'So I took a long breath. Inside, I was terrified, I was aware of my heart beating fast, but I thought *I can deal with this, he's just another fat boy bully, he's like those pumped-up little Hitlers I remember from the Brotherhood*. I stood up so that we were eye to eye. Actually, I'm taller than he is so that helped. I used the feedback formula we rehearsed and told him that of course he was entitled to his opinion about the evidence I had offered. I told him that getting up and physically coming so close felt like menace. I held up my hand and told him to back off, that he was frightening me, that it was wrong, that he should use my proper name, not a demeaning nickname, and that my request to him was never to do that again. Then I paused for him to reply.'

The atmosphere in the room was charged. She said, 'People seemed as if they were hardly breathing.' A purple flush suffused the boss's face, then he said, 'Just a joke, just a joke – you've got to be able to take a joke, young lady!'

Rachel had resumed her seat.

I commented that many people, mouselike or not, would have run out of the room, but she had stayed until the meeting was over.

'And now?' I asked.

'And now I'm definitely on the search for another job, but he's not going to force me out, I'm going to take my time.'

News of this event spread at speed. I knew that people would be watching and waiting. The story joined my own private list of five-star awards for client courage. It would join the one where the client running a microbusiness had refused to be bullied by threats of legal action from one of the richest men in the world after he had pretended there was a flaw in her work and had refused to pay her invoice. It would join another where a young woman chief executive had told a much older and more power-ful chairman during a crisis for the organization that if either of them were to leave their jobs it would be the chairman and not her. And yet another where a chief executive with terminal cancer had carried on with her job until just a few days before her death.

My programme with Rachel was coming to an end and as we said our goodbyes, we promised to keep in touch.

Reports began to steal into the business press about the organization. What had previously seemed an uncrackable model for success and relentless expansion appeared, initially, to be merely faltering. Then it swiftly tumbled into meltdown as its customers fled to competitors. The darling of the City was now the subject of harshly critical analysis and it issued a profits warning. A witty and anonymous insider was writing a blog exposing some of the less impressive aspects of the culture, including its tendency towards heavy-handed top-down control, coercion, overt sexism and bullying. Within a few months, many of the senior team had 'stepped down', including Rachel's boss and the HR director who had asked me to undertake the coaching work with her. A new chief executive was hired to lead the process of salvage and renewal.

A few years later one of Rachel's regular emails told me she was doing a training course to qualify as a coach and one of my books about coaching was on the reading list. I was delighted to agree to her suggestion that we might get together over a cup of coffee for a catch-up.

'Those sessions with you convinced me that, yes, I could do boss behaviour, and no, I didn't want to be a boss. After all the hoo-ha of the crisis, the new chief exec offered me the job of leading the culture change programme, but I turned it down. It would have meant running a big team and I didn't want it,' she said. 'I realized I didn't have to do it in the oppressive way I'd seen all around me, but that was quite separate from understanding that being a manager was not something I wanted to do.'

Rachel did need to learn what delegation was and to acquire that useful feedback framework, but I had not, as I had thought, been equipping her to become a more effective leader. Instead Rachel had realized that her interest was in organization behaviour and in what she called 'moral leadership'. 'I'd had an advanced-level personal experience as a kid in how dysfunctional groups work, I'd seen at close quarters what keeps people in them, and then I saw it again as an adult.'

Rachel was well into a career as a freelance facilitator and team coach where her many strengths and skills could have full play. Her extensive knowledge of group behaviour and her commitment to openness combined with her charm and persuasiveness were exactly what was needed in this role. 'I'm not afraid of any of those chief executives, including some of those grossly overpaid people in the FTSE 100,' she said, smiling happily. 'They pay me premium rates because I can tell them frankly what's going on all around them that they can't seem to see for themselves. I use that feedback stuff all the time with groups, and you know what? They take it meekly! Of course they do!'

The truth was that she never had been Little Miss Mouse. It was the organization and its culture that was dysfunctional, not Rachel.

Endings

A Little Piece of Theatre

Outside, the afternoon was darkening and the promised icy rain had begun. Inside, it began to feel a little cool. I was working at a business centre where they rented out small meeting rooms. Sometimes I had a suspicion that to save money they turned the heating down to a slightly less than comfortable level.

There was a rap on the door and Alex, William's wife, stepped into the room. Chilly air rushed in with her and the fur collar of her coat was slick with melted sleet. I stood to welcome her and to offer a hot drink from the flasks on the side table.

'Not for me, thanks.' She shucked off her coat. 'It would be a distraction from our main business.'

It is unusual though not entirely unheard of for a client to ask if a third party can be included in a coaching session, normally as a one-off event. A woman chief executive wanted to bring a member of her team to one of our meetings because she was finding him 'dismissive and arrogant' while being aware that, as one half of the relationship, she probably had at least some responsibility for its prickly state. Domestic issues are often present in a coaching conversation, even if they are rarely explored in detail.

The third party is usually wary about these events. They will understand that as a coach your essential loyalty is to your client. They will guess that they will have been discussed, not necessarily in flattering terms, and that the client may have shared uncomfortable secrets about the relationship. When I meet such third parties, I am clear with them and with myself that I am not there to do mediation. This would be impossible since I have not been freely chosen by both equally. Posing as a mediator or a couples therapist would inevitably involve pretence, careful 'forgetting' of vital information and potentially a fast track to duplicitous conduct. To make this clear I like to make a phone call, ideally on speakerphone in the presence of the client, while I discuss why he or she has asked for the session, what the purpose of the proposed joint coaching conversation is, exploring how willing the other party is to attend, what they might want to get out of it and what they expect my role to be.

That's the theory. In this case the conversation with Alex had not happened, despite my repeated attempts to contact her. William assured me that she understood the limits and terms of the engagement and was eager to join us.

His wish to involve her was linked to his reason for requesting coaching in the first place. William's company was poised for rapid growth. They were ready to open an office in Los Angeles and William had been asked to lead what was planned as an ambitious expansion into the US market. Saying yes would mean moving and then staying for at least three years.

As a piece of coaching, this had a brisk, brief flavour, just six sessions, and the commission from William's boss was to work with him to facilitate the decision.

'He's dithering and I'm puzzled about why. If he doesn't go, he will have a job here for as long as he wants it, and maybe he's holding out to be my successor, though I doubt that. Probably he should make a move of some kind, for his own development as much as anything else. I can't prise any more out of him and I think he needs a coach. It can't go on like this. He needs to decide one way or the other.'

I had asked William a number of questions which had all had the same underlying themes: 'Where are you in your life and career? How do you feel about your current job?'

'Mmmm. I enjoy my job, but I've been doing it for a while. It could be a good opportunity to make a change before I get bored.'

It was a half-hearted reply, but it is not unusual for people to talk about such life-changing decisions with what seems like half-heartedness. I told myself that William perhaps had the judicious, equable temperament that could be mistaken for lack of enthusiasm and that there was no need to read too much into it.

In theory it looked like an ideal time to make a move. Their daughter had left home. The mortgage was paid off, there were investments, there was a secure pension. William had been discreet about his marriage, but it sounded from his accounts like a friendly and collaborative relationship. We had discussed the many pluses and the few minuses of moving to LA. The pluses were the thrill of running his own operation after some years of being the number two, and the stimulus of working in a vibrant American city. Against that were the upheaval of moving to a new country and the concerns about leaping into the unknown. It seemed perfectly understandable that William wanted to include his wife in our discussions. Moving would mean that she would have to disrupt her own career as an expert in ancient history at a leading British university.

It is inevitable as a coach that you feel more connection with some clients than with others. In William's case we quickly discovered we had grown up in the same part of the same Welsh city and in suburban houses that could have been identical twins. He had been taught maths by my stepbrother-in-law, he had been at school with one of my cousins. My mother, ever conscious of the need to watch the pennies, had for certain bought goods from his father's market stall. We had both left home at eighteen never to return for anything more than brief stays. Years of living in England meant we had each somehow lost our local accents though we were both able to hear the faintest of echoes in the other's speech. We were both the first in our families to go to university and to establish a professional career rather than working in a shop or in a humble admin job.

It is daunting to take risks that involve overcoming what we dread. We can all feel preprogrammed to seek the easy options and to meet fear with avoidance. My parents had made this bargain: security would always matter more to them than personal growth. My father was unemployed and virtually penniless for several years throughout a long economic depression. He and my mother were in their late thirties when they eventually felt able to afford marriage. My mother, the eldest in a hard-up family, had been sent out to work at fourteen. My father's family had squandered their money and his education, too, had ended brutally and too soon. My parents had been hurt by repeated shocks and by events where they had had no possibility of control. Their fear of poverty drove them to emphasize caution and modesty. They were ambitious for me, their only child, but their ambitions were limited. These were: do well at school, go to university then come back to live near us with a nice safe job as a teacher, live in a house just like ours, marry another teacher, keep your house tidy, give up work when you have those two polite children, share our political values and cultural beliefs and, above all, never do anything that upsets the status quo. They conveyed this to protect me. It was done from love and kindness.

Although he was some years younger than me, William's story had been similar. As a graduate with one of the first British degrees in computing, he had moved from IBM to a series of software houses and had been one of the first employees in the company where he now worked, rising effortlessly to its senior ranks as a liked and respected leader.

Slowly, as our sessions continued, I was concluding that this was a bigger decision for William than it seemed. If you were to ask a typical British senior manager whether they would like a relatively easy and pain-free move to LA for a few years, my assumption is that the majority would have no difficulty in saying yes. Yet there was some diffidence for William, more reluctance than seemed justified by the circumstances.

'What is this hesitation about?' I asked. 'Is it some version of that stuff you and I grew up with? Fear of leaving the safety of the known and predictable?'

William gave a little grimace. We had often been able to talk in shorthand about the stifling yet comforting nature of what he had dubbed 'Cardiff Conformity'.

'I don't think it's that. But it would mean not seeing my daughter, missing my close friends, and it's a big ask for my wife because she would probably feel she was being uprooted. It would be difficult. She works in a pretty specialist field. And I'm not sure about the US. I think of myself as European rather than just British. I enjoy being able to pop over to Paris or Brussels, I love the London cultural scene – all our wonderful restaurants, all that music, film and theatre on tap.'

We had rehearsed these arguments yet again in the hour before Alex joined us.

Now she moved to sit down. Someone from the business centre had carefully chosen the circular table to be desk height, big enough for three or four people to have a meeting so that their elbows would not be touching yet close enough to feel connected.

Alex took her time to settle into her chair. She was poised and calm.

'Thanks for coming, Alex,' I said. 'It's a pleasure to meet you. William thought it would be a good idea to involve you in the coaching discussion, but before we begin, is there anything you'd like to raise, for instance –'

Alex held up a hand like a traffic cop to cut across my little speech. 'No, there isn't. Let's get to the point.'

She turned to her husband and from that moment on never addressed another word to me.

'William. This offer has come up. You may decide to take it. You may not. It's up to you. If you do, I won't be coming with you. You know as well as I do that our marriage is a sham and has been for a long time. No sex for – how long? Ten years at least. At first you made excuses but then you didn't bother. We've been living parallel lives. I'd sort of pieced it together anyway but then someone we both know saw you in Amsterdam. You remember you said you were going to that conference? You weren't at the conference because there wasn't a conference, but this person saw you in a gay bar canoodling with Gary, the special friend who it turns out really is a special friend. We can get a quick divorce, divide everything fifty-fifty and go our separate ways. I wish you'd been honest with me, but there it is, you haven't been.'

She paused. She was relaxed and alert, her voice steady. She smiled at him pleasantly. 'I will be starting a new life too and I wish you well.'

William was motionless. His face was frozen.

I was faintly aware that snow was now falling outside, making soft arcs against the black of the windowpanes, and that I could no longer hear the traffic for the deep hush in the room.

Alex stood up, taking her time, hands lightly touching the table. She leant a little towards William. 'We can talk about how we make it happen this evening at home.' She nodded to me, picked up her coat, tossed it casually over her shoulders and swept out of the room. She had been with us for five minutes at most. The door clicked shut behind her.

When I talk to gay friends and clients about coming out, they often tell me that for some gay people it is still alarming, a task to be endlessly postponed. I have a friend, now in his forties, whose parents still speak of their hope that he will meet 'the right girl', shyly mentioning yet again their yearning for grandchildren. He believes they could not cope with knowing that he is gay. Coming out can still be a challenge even in the era of joyful gay marriages, gay couples raising children, equality legislation and openly gay politicians.

At our next session a few weeks later, William described himself as 'sheepish and guilty', apprehensive that I was judging him harshly for being less than frank with me, for hiding his sexuality and for deceiving his wife. I was not judging him in this way. I remembered all too clearly the phobias, disdain, whispering and coded references around homosexuality as I was growing up in Cardiff. I remembered my own naive belief, thanks to the way it was represented then on TV, that the only way to recognize a gay man was from his camp appearance and mannerisms. I remembered why I had been so pleased to get away.

My instinct that there was fear and avoidance involved for William in making the decision had been correct, but I had been completely wrong about the cause. And now another connection had occurred to me.

'You must have known Andrew T – at school,' I said.

William bit his lip and I could not read his face. 'I did, though he was a few years ahead of me at school. Why do you ask?'

Andrew was the son of a neighbour. We had been in the same loose gang of local children who played out in the neighbourhood park, building dens, climbing trees, staging tennis tournaments in a road that had few cars, along with various other pranks that would have today's parents aghast at the lack of adult supervision. As a teenager, Andrew's sexuality became obvious since he did nothing to disguise it. I loved his company, admired his overt snubs to the dull suburban canopy under which we both lived and was in awe of his ambition to become an actor. I had admired his brazen flamboyance and had kept loosely in touch with him when we both eventually moved to London. He was one of the first British men to die of AIDS.

As I explained this, I realized that we both had unshed tears in our eyes.

William said, 'He was one of the funniest, loveliest people I've ever met. But I couldn't do that gay-scene-queer-pride thing, it just isn't me. I often think of him. He used to tell me to man up, teasing me, daring me to acknowledge our friendship, but I couldn't. His terrible illness . . . it took him such a long time to die. Being gay seemed like a death sentence then. It frightened me.'

'Did you know,' I asked, 'that his mother maintained to the end of her life that his partner was "a flatmate" and that he had died of pneumonia? She just couldn't face the truth.'

'I didn't, but yeah, Cardiff Conformity in action yet again.'

When the kaleidoscope of our lives is given such a sharp tap it is never the case that the pieces fall back into the same pattern. William did not move to L A and the relationship with Gary, his long-standing lover, did not survive its exposure. The divorce was amicable and swift. Alex had cherished a private wish to become what she called 'a proper gallery curator' but realized this was unlikely to be an achievable ambition for a woman in her late forties. Instead she became the partner in life as well as in business of an international dealer in antiquities, moving to the US herself. Possibly this man had long been part of the parallel existence she had described at our meeting, but that was just my guess.

I asked William at our final session what he thought explained Alex's extraordinary decision to announce the abrupt severance of their marriage at that coaching session.

He shrugged. 'She's always been one for dramatic gestures and she's always loved an audience,' he said. 'Getting her own back maybe? Taking control because she had felt humiliated? I don't know and I haven't asked. I didn't see it as hostile really. I've always admired her chutzpah and flair, and I still do. She represents the opposite of Cardiff Conformity to me and that was what attracted me to her in the first place. I really did love her, you do know that? And I still do. We'll always be friends, despite everything.'

I nodded. I could see that this was true.

He gazed at me thoughtfully, then added, eyes glowing, 'But as a little piece of theatre, you have to agree, wasn't it just perfect?'

Pretending the World is Funny

Even though I insisted that Jackson and I went through some kind of meet-and-match event, it was clear from his demeanour that it was a done deal as far as he was concerned. I liked him immediately, a big presence in every way: tall, bulky, smiley, boyish. He had heard about me from a medical colleague in another hospital. 'I blustered my way through HR to make this happen,' he boomed cheerfully, 'even though you weren't on their bureaucratically meticulous and tediously administered list of approved suppliers and in theory I'm not senior enough to deserve it.'

The agenda seemed familiar enough from coaching I had done with other doctors. At its heart was how to improve relationships with senior colleagues in the hospital. There were plenty of signs that this was not going well. Although there is now much more training to equip clinicians with these skills, many report finding it challenging. I had one clinical director client whose issue was how to get three warring surgeons in the same department to talk to each other. Patient safety was being compromised by their bickering and two of them had not spoken for five years. It had simply never occurred to her that she might talk privately to each about how they viewed the problem, then call a meeting, chair it and openly negotiate a solution with the three men concerned. In another hospital I worked as coach to its executive team where the medical director, a pleasant man new to his role, had no idea how annoying it was to his colleagues that he turned up to executive team meetings wearing scrubs and a stethoscope, even though he was not on call that day.

In our first session I heard something of Jackson's life story. When you work with doctors you discover how often it seems to be the case that there are family traditions about going into medicine. Jackson's grandfather and both parents had been doctors; he had cousins, uncles and aunts who were doctors. Few of these doctors describe any overt pressure to join the profession, it comes to seem like a natural choice.

Jackson's parents were busy and preoccupied. His poignant description of his parents was that they were well meaning but emotionally cool: 'I was loved but not quite loved.' He said that contact with them was mostly about pressure to get top marks at school: 'If you got 99 per cent the question was why wasn't it 100 per cent?' He was an only child and was sent to a boys' boarding school at eight years old. As he described this life-changing event, he kept his smile while telling me it was inexplicable to him that his father had been miserable at this school yet had chosen to inflict the same misery on him. It had been put to him that getting the best possible education was more important than what was assumed to be the fleeting distress of settling in to a place with so many advantages. Jackson described crying himself to sleep every night for his first few weeks and then slowly adjusting.

I asked, 'How did you do that adjusting?'

'I did what every other boy there did if you didn't want to be bullied, I just shut myself down. I hid the teddy bear. No one was going to help me so I had to stop feeling anything. There were a few teachers who took an interest and were nice to me. I found I could make people laugh and that was my way of surviving.'

'And what's been the impact on you of that experience?'

Jackson knew the theory. Sending young boys to boarding schools has been described as 'privileged abandonment'. Separated unnaturally early from their families, these children have to become faux adults who must never, ever show weakness or emotion and always appear more confident than they feel. He guffawed. 'I'm your classic frozen English ex-public schoolboy, I daresay. With a secret teddy bear on my bed!'

Was the teddy bear reference a joke or a statement of fact? Jackson winked and told me I'd have to work that out for myself.

It is embarrassing for a doctor to be overweight. Doctors are conscious that they should be setting a virtuous example. In discussing his health as part of our scan of everything else that was going on in his life, Jackson said that what he called 'fighting the flab' had been a constant battle since his late twenties. He showed me the food diary he had been keeping as part of his attempt to lose weight. This revealed in frank detail the massive canteen breakfasts gulped down in a hurry before starting a ward round or clinic, the innumerable bags of crisps, lunches with chips, the many beers with casual friends after work. He said, 'I'm tired all the time – I need to see a doctor!'

Jackson had just split up from his long-term partner. He said the relationship had been celibate for several years. 'She can't bear me to touch her, but I still love her madly.'

He told me about what he called 'Jackson's Jamboree Jollies'. These were medical conferences all over the world usually sponsored by drug companies. He welcomed the long-haul flights and the anonymous hotel rooms because they were opportunities to eat and drink uninhibited by the risk of anyone knowing him or criticizing. Since splitting up with his partner, it had been appealing to accept every such invitation. Food was a consolation. Alcohol provided what he called 'short-term anaesthesia' followed by shame over what he described as 'my disgusting guzzling'.

Feedback from colleagues revealed that Jackson was popular, confident and knowledgeable in his specialism. People enjoyed his friendliness and good humour. Several said he was an inveterate joke-teller, luring you in with, 'I was leaving my flat this morning when . . .' In his role as teacher and trainer he favoured generous humour, with himself as the fall guy and supportive questioner. This attitude coaxed right answers and inspired guesses from nervous young medical students. People also said they found him loud, and thought he was probably unaware that he seemed to draw attention to himself to the point where no other conversation could go on in any room that contained him. They loved his cleverness, his ability to come up with innovative ideas for patient care and for reforming systems. They thought he might need to learn some new influencing tactics around senior academic colleagues, reporting that he was surprisingly over-deferential to them, especially if they were men. Some commented thoughtfully that they did not know who he really was, found it odd that he said nothing about his private life, wondered if he had close friends rather than drinking buddies and speculated that he might be lonely and vulnerable.

I, too, saw that vulnerability. I thought I recognized the lonely, not-quite-loved small boy in the successful, popular doctor. I was touched by his willingness to confide in me. He had embarked on a professional relationship with me based merely on the flimsiness of a recommendation from a colleague. When I commented on this, he said, 'I thought I may as well give it my all and tell you everything, otherwise I'm not going to get anything out of it.'

The coaching programme seemed to go well. We worked on influencing tactics, on how to overcome fear of those powerful male academic colleagues who, as he was the first to point out, reminded him of his father. We looked at how to soft-pedal his alleged 'loudness' and how to get the maximum advantage from his many strengths, including his gifts as a teacher.

As this work progressed, it became apparent that Jackson also had some bothersome career issues. He could easily have continued on a successful clinical career, perhaps moving up the medical managerial hierarchy. But he valued his research and teaching. He said he yearned to get further recognition in a medical school but to do that he needed to boost his credibility through certain honorary positions, for instance joining a national committee or becoming the editor of an academic journal in his specialism. Just before we had started our work together, he had been turned down for roles in both. The post-interview feedback was mostly too thin to be helpful but there were some hints that he had not listened carefully enough to the questions and had offered answers that were too rambling and perhaps contained too many jokes. We agreed that if new possibilities occurred here, I would work with him on how to improve his interview technique.

One quiet Sunday afternoon my mobile rang and I saw that it was Jackson. I give my number to clients freely. Without exception they respect my weekends and evenings. It would have to be something vitally important for this unstated rule to be breached.

'Jenny? Well, that pharmaceutical company should be sued.' There was humour in his voice even though he sounded husky and slow. 'I took what I thought was a proper overdose and I seem to have been asleep or unconscious for twenty-four hours, but, ha ha, I'm still here!'

Even now, writing many years later, I can feel my intense shock. I could not take it in. I thought I had misheard. I don't remember my immediate words, but I do remember stuttering with disbelief.

Then, 'You took . . . an overdose?'

'Yes. I thought I'd had enough really. I'm just a nuisance. I'm a complete arse as a human being. I'm no good. Better to end it. No one would miss me.'

Much of the rest of the conversation is a blur, but I do recall establishing the circumstances: heavy drinking alone at home in the anonymous new flat, then cramming pills into his mouth and settling down to die. I remember assuring him of how many people would have missed him. I told him how much I liked him and of how painful his death would have been for me. He told me that the decision to take his life had been building for a long time.

'I messed up the most important relationship in my life and I don't know what I did or why she won't love me. I'm a disappointment to my parents. I'm fat and ugly, I let myself down. I'm exhausted all the time and I'm letting my patients down too. So many of them are never going to get better anyway. I always thought being a doctor was about curing the sick, but if people are too sick to cure, it's so depressing seeing them die on you, you just feel helpless. It's not why I went into medicine . . .'

We talked for more than an hour. As I steadied myself down I realized I had to persuade Jackson to get help. Aware that I had absolutely no means of enforcing this, I asked him to promise me he would go to his GP the next day, say what had happened and seek a fast-track referral to a mental health professional. Doctors often prefer self-medicating or casually asking a colleague for help to seeing another doctor for a proper consultation. If you are a hospital-based doctor you may believe the myth that GPs are people who are not as clever as you. Many such doctors do not bother to register with a general practice. Jackson did have a GP – in theory.

'All the GPs there are idiots,' he said.

'What – all of them? Are you sure?'

'Well, there might be one who's slightly less of an idiot than the others.'

'So you might be able to trust this one who's slightly less of an idiot?'

Grudgingly, Jackson agreed this was possible and agreed to call the practice first thing the next day.

I asked him what his plan was to stay safe from self-harm, including destroying any remaining stash of pills. He promised me he would flush them away as soon as our conversation had ended.

Doctors make for awkward patients. Their training encourages them to see themselves as special. There is the country of the sick and then there are the doctors, a superior caste. Being over-dedicated to your work is admired in medicine and medical education often dissociates mind and spirit from body. Asking for help can be seen as weakness. Doctors often refuse to surrender to their illnesses, carrying on even when clearly very unwell, ignoring symptoms which would demand immediate treatment if seen in their patients. Many doctors view their own illnesses as a failure of will, a moral lapse, and such doctors do not look after themselves or each other. Nowhere is this truer than where the question is mental health. Doctors have the same rates of all the common mental illnesses as the general population, but many studies of doctor health have shown that doctors feel particular shame about seeking help with mental illness or with addictions to drugs and alcohol. Their fear of being judged and stigmatized is severe, made worse by worries about whether owning up to mental illness would compromise their careers. Add to this the fact that doctors are working with anxious people and sick people yet are told to stay objective with little or no provision to unload their own feelings.

Being a doctor is demanding. The Covid pandemic highlighted the need for unrelenting commitment, long hours and the ability to steel yourself for disappointment. They may also experience 'moral injury', the term first used to describe trauma-related symptoms in military personnel returning from the Vietnam War where people felt they had been forced into actions which had profoundly breached their moral codes. For doctors this might include feeling obliged to ignore the needs of patients whose lives appeared to be of lesser value, for instance, denying an elderly patient a ventilator. There is a high rate of suicide in doctors. Apart from the stresses of their profession, there is a familiarity with death or violence and easy access to the means of ending their own life.

I told Jackson I would call him again that day and did so three times just to check on how he was feeling. I got blandly reassuring answers. He said he had disposed of the remaining pills.

I called him every day the following week. He had fulfilled the promise to consult his GP and had had a fast-track referral to someone he described as a 'counsellor'. Troubled by this, I asked why he was not seeing a psychiatrist or psychotherapist. His reply was that it would be 'too embarrassing' to see another doctor.

'In any case,' he said, 'isn't it true that all psychiatrists are bat-shit crazy and that's why they're psychiatrists?'

I was thoroughly frightened by this conversation, consulted another experienced coach and realized I knew little about how to deal with suicide. Within a few weeks I had enrolled with a suicide prevention charity as a potential volunteer. The training showed me that this role was not for me, but I did learn how to spot suicidal thinking and to recognize the falsity of so many of the myths about suicide, such as the one about a failed attempt being 'merely a cry for help' or that people who make one attempt are unlikely to make another. One failed attempt is a reliable indicator that others may follow, including an attempt that succeeds. I learnt to face my worry that exploring the wish to die would make an actual suicide more likely, whereas the truth is that the most helpful thing you can do is to enquire into the person's feelings about their possible suicide. Picking up on vague statements such as 'My life is not worth living', or frequent talk about funerals, wills and death, or unusual 'goodbye' conversations is vital. These are hints that need exploring, not brushing over. This needs nerve. It needs determination because you have to get over your fear of embarrassing yourself or the other person. As a coach you need reassurance that this is the right thing to do because, unlike anything else in coaching, someone's life could be at stake.

Jackson finished his six sessions of counselling and was put on antidepressants by his GP. Privately, I thought this seemed superficial and far too short a treatment, but he assured me he was feeling well and, against my better judgement, I believed him. He asked his organization for a three-month extension of his coaching programme. We spent most of it on how he might manage his stress better by making more realistic assumptions about what it was possible to achieve. Our agenda also included finding another rewarding relationship with a woman, getting his weight back under control, taking more exercise, rebuilding the relationship with his parents and using his considerable networking skills to secure the career recognition that he sought.

Many of these goals were achieved. Internet dating did not produce a soulmate, but it did mean introductions to several pleasant and attractive women. Jackson shed thirty pounds easily and his alcohol consumption dropped dramatically. In describing his weight loss, Jackson showed me his meticulously charted progress. His data included standard deviations, correlations with exercise and a lot more obsessive detail. I duly admired all of it. He did get to join a national advisory committee.

I was aware there was real liking between us and once it was clear that the coaching was over, Jackson hovered somewhere on the cloudy borderline of becoming a friend. I invited him to a social event where he was the star of the evening, taking part in a silly game which required advanced clowning skills. He invited me to dinner where the meal turned into informal coaching for a forthcoming interview.

Then there was silence. My emails to his personal address or through LinkedIn went unanswered. At this time I had major life upheavals of my own to negotiate. It had become too difficult to manage the flimsy boundaries between work and home where my husband and I were running the same company along with a co-director. I left the payroll to start up again on my own. After my husband died, coping with the painful aftermath of bereavement, I decided to restrict my work to three days a week. I had little emotional or physical energy to spare. But every so often I sent another email to Jackson, hoping for the usual breezy reply.

Several months later, beginning to recover from my own crises, I was seriously puzzled – and alarmed. It did not seem like him not to contact me. Where were those promised 'mildly boozy evenings in a nice wine bar' or at the Comedy Store? I had no contacts at his hospital but knew their website would list senior staff.

His name was not there.

Jackson had taken his own life a few months after our coaching had finished. He had left no note. No one had an explanation. I had missed it all: the appalled shock and hurt of his friends, colleagues and patients, the tributes, the post-mortem, the inquest. Their sorrow was matched by their bewilderment. How could such an overtly cheerful person have been so unhappy without anyone spotting it?

A suicide leaves everyone close to the dead person with the question 'Why?' Anger is common: how dared they have done this? What gave them the right to walk into that void? Often this phase is followed by guilt: at failure to say words that might have been spoken, help that might have been given, hints that might have been spotted. I felt much of this. I felt I had lost someone I had liked enormously and who had been on his way to becoming a good friend. I felt I had let Jackson down and that I should have been more persistent in my attempts to keep in touch. I felt furious that his death seemed to demonstrate that misery can triumph over optimism. I felt the things that people feel when there has been a suicide in their lives.

I am not so naive as to think I could have prevented this tragedy. But the relationship was important enough for him to call me on that Sunday afternoon. While we were working together as coach and client it is possible that I was providing some sort of protective shield. He did allow me to see behind the cheerful but exhausting mask which had fooled most people for most of his life. But our connection did not seem to have been strong enough to survive the formal end of the coaching. Jackson probably believed that he did not deserve to be loved. Possibly he believed that our relationship depended on money changing hands. In the beginning it did, later I did not think so, but maybe he had disagreed.

I understand now that suicide is common and how many people's lives it touches. Just in the last few weeks while writing this story there has been a client who told me as part of our first meeting that two teenagers in her extended family had taken their own lives; another whose first husband had not been able to face his secret debts and had hanged himself; a client whose childhood had been devastated by the frequent suicide attempts made by her mother; a client whose husband is showing worrying signs that suicide is something he is considering; a close friend whose sibling took his own life. I will now notice immediately if a client expresses potentially suicidal thoughts to me. These are no longer taboo topics. It is safe to discuss and to explore and to strongly encourage access to treatment.

I have had many clients over the years who have appeared to be without any outer layer of resilience. Their vulnerability is obvious and sometimes their helplessness seems to invite other people's cruelty. Then there are people like Jackson who have created a mask so convincing that no one sees the raw hurt underneath. Real contentment lies somewhere between these extremes. If you train people to think of you as a happy clown you will have to bellow to get their attention when you need it. If you seem too needy, there will be plenty of people who will give you a kicking.

Like many comedians, amateur and professional, Jackson was preoccupied by instability. His jokes were attempts to master a wobbly reality. I realize now that he subtly drew my attention to the way his behaviour was a faint shadow from the long tradition of tragic clowns. We frequently spent a few minutes talking about TV or films at the beginning of our sessions and comedy was a theme that popped up often, including discussing some of the brilliant inventions of Steve Coogan as Alan Partridge or Ricky Gervais as David Brent. These both drew on the character created by Tony Hancock, a successful British comedian of the 1950s and '60s. With characters like Hancock, Alan Partridge and David Brent, the entire comedy rests on the unease we feel at characters who do not know how ridiculous they seem to other people, yet at some level they understand that something is wrong. We are torn between laughter and embarrassment watching them, seeing that they struggle to manage themselves by pretending the world is funny. Tony Hancock took his own life in 1968.

I remember Jackson often. I wonder if he died with his teddy beside him, believing, against all the evidence, that his life was worthless. When I think of him, I feel a stab of sadness at the needless loss of a life, an outstanding doctor, a client, a friend.

Death Coaching

'Do you do death coaching?'

The voice was light, sharp and amused, and I did not recognize it straight away.

'It's Ben – remember? The "Emotional Dinosaur" from that team coaching you did a few years ago.'

Then I did remember. The label 'Emotional Dinosaur' had been given him by an exasperated colleague during a session where we had been exploring why it was that this newly formed team was so reluctant to acknowledge each other's stress. There had been a vigorous discussion about what 'emotional intelligence' really was and why it mattered. Ben had become notorious in this group for expressing the view, most definitely tongue in cheek, that they were scientists, the rational mind was the only thing that mattered and emotion was for people who were 'big girls' blouses'.

This event was one of a series with that team. Ben was only one of several whose initial fear of exposure, or of seeming 'weak', led to many semi-serious jokes to me, the only non-scientist present, about how they were always expecting that at any moment I would be asking them to do 'Tibetan chanting sitting on beanbags'. One person did actually sit on a beanbag but that was because her excruciating back pain was being made so much worse by the silly little gilt chairs which the hotel had provided for the event.

I did take one calculated risk with this team, but by that much later stage they were comfortable with each other. This was to do a guided meditation, asking them each to imagine themselves in a calm, special place where they were always happy. Then I invited them to see their future selves walking towards them with a message on how to live a more relaxed and fulfilling life in the present.

I remembered that despite his apparent commitment to such a pre-neuroscience view of the human brain, Ben was popular with his colleagues. I had liked him too. Over a series of two-day residential events I had been pleased if I found myself sitting next to him at dinner. The exchange was always stimulating and fun. In one of these conversations he had asked me how I described myself. Did I, for instance, call myself a life coach? I had explained my visceral response to the phrase 'life coach', since, maybe unfairly, it suggested a credulous person who enrols for a one-off 'become a coach' weekend course, the only requirements being that you 'like people' and are prepared to part with a large sum of money. You would then find that the platitudinous simplicities you had been shown on the course did not equip you in any way for the actual complexities of coaching. You would find there were few takers for 'life coaching', as opposed to the world of executive coaching where you were expected to be able to cope with anything on the 'life' agenda as well as understanding the byzantine complexities of organization behaviour. Ben had seen how his question had created a pleasingly intense response, one perhaps connected with the possibility of protesting too much. After that he had taken delight in talking of me in public as 'the team's life coach'.

We had also had a more serious conversation where we had discussed the differences between coaching and psychoanalysis. I had expressed the view that all coaches owe a debt to Sigmund Freud with his emphasis on the importance of childhood in shaping us and in revealing the role of the unconscious mind. I described Freud's house in London, now a modest museum and one of my favourite places to visit. You can see his richly ornamented consulting room, including his couch and chair, the room looking for all the world as though he has just popped away for a moment, maybe to let out his beloved dog, Yofi. None-theless, I had stressed that psychoanalysis is a very different process because it tries to answer the question 'Why?' as in 'Why do I always feel like this? Why can't I forget the past?' whereas coaches are more interested in the question 'What?' as in 'What should I do?'

Back in the present, I was startled by his question.

'Do I do death coaching? I don't think so but tell me more.'

Still maintaining his light tone, Ben told me he had been diagnosed with a rare form of lung cancer despite never hav-ing smoked and never having lived with a smoker. The possible cause was exposure to a range of chemicals at the industrial plant where he had worked as a young graduate. His illness was ter-minal. Palliative care was all that was possible and he had at most eighteen months to live.

I was saddened. I remembered Ben as a lean, youthful-looking family man, a keen marathon runner, working long hours, for-midably committed to his particular area of research and at the peak of a distinguished career.

After a few more quiet minutes of commiseration, I said, 'This sounds like a case for counselling not coaching.'

'Yes, I thought you'd say that. The hospital offered me coun-selling and I went to one session. The woman sat there with her head cocked to one side all the time like a bird listening for worms and exuding excessive sorrow on my behalf. I came out of it feeling like I'd been in a bath of warm sludge. It didn't help.'

'You had an unfortunate experience there – maybe therapy would be a better bet?'

'No. I don't want to sit for hours talking about my childhood. The oncology team at the hospital are fantastic anyway. They're always there with information, very sensitive, kindness itself and never rushing me.'

I reminded him of our earlier conversation and explained that many therapists did not take the psycho-dynamic approach of enquiring into childhood and that I could recommend two or three whom I thought would do a good job, including one whose client I had been myself. Ben agreed they might indeed be excellent, but insisted that what he wanted was coaching and that he wanted to be coached by me because we would not need to do what he called 'wasting time' on getting to know each other and that he trusted me to be able to get straight to the point.

'And what is that point?'

'I need to plan for my death and there's no one in my life I can do that with. It has to be someone outside my family and friends.'

I said, 'If I feel out of my depth, or that I'm not serving your best interests, or if you experience any variant of warm sludge or clumsy attempts at amateur psychoanalysis or anything else that feels wrong, then we have to agree to discuss it and maybe to stop. I'd refer you to someone else if that's what you wanted.'

I felt we had an honest agreement, judicious enough to keep me calm at entering unknown territory. I reminded myself of my own guidelines about the principles of coaching, none of which involves being an expert on the subjects the client brings and where the core assumption is that the client has the resourcefulness to deal with their own problems.

Ben had estimated that we might need six sessions. He had made a list of topics. This started with how to handle colleagues, went on to what he called 'practicalities' such as making a will, and ended with designing a memorial event. He explained that my role was to offer perspective and to give him 'a kick up the arse' if he failed to deliver on any of the actions we agreed at the end of each session.

So we began.

'How do I deal with these people at work who shuffle and look away? Some of them, and I thought they were friends, see me coming and immediately dodge out of sight.' This was one of the few times in our sessions where Ben became agitated. 'Why are they so cowardly?'

We explored the evident unfairness of this: the person who is ill has to manage the embarrassment of the fit and healthy rather than the other way round. But that's the way it is. So many of us lack resolve in the face of other people's hurt, loss and sadness. Together, Ben and I developed and rehearsed a pocket-sized performance which involved consciously seeking people out, including those who gave every sign of wanting to run away. He would then deliver a 'script' in which he acknowledged the terminal nature of the diagnosis, told them he planned to work for as long as possible, gave them an update on his treatment, and would then resolutely change the subject and edge purposefully away. There was an optional extra for those super-annoying people who, unbidden, offered recommendations involving top-secret pills which could only be bought through the dark web or interventions through prayer and faith healing. There were also all the would-be counsellors and self-labelled 'intuitives' who said things like, 'Please do have my mobile number, any time you want to talk, day or night, I'll be there . . .' Instead of feeling patronized, looking annoyed and making off as quickly as possible, Ben developed a smooth little speech of thanks. He would reassure them that he already had professional support and had no need of more.

In subsequent sessions we discussed finding the right solicitor to update his will and what kinds of amendments he would need to make after discussions with his wife, including some bequests for godchildren. He recorded a video for each of his children, to be played when they reached eighteen. He added Power of Attorney for health and welfare to his legal list as a way of making his wishes clear if he were to lose the mental capacity to make his own decisions about end-of-life care. He reported back on a visit to a hospice, saying that the moment he entered it he had felt serenity, seeing it as a place full of light, views of trees and cheerful staff.

We discussed his intellectual legacy – his achievements and his pride in his personal and professional life.

'How would you like these to be represented in your obituaries?'

Ben looked startled for a moment. He was a modest man, but I knew that there would be interest in his death.

'Can you plan these things?'

I explained that some people choose their obituary writers, often close friends who could be supplied with crucial dates and who could ask what particular aspects of a life the subject would like emphasized. Ben was amused by this idea, taking it one step further in asking the chosen writers, who both agreed immediately, to send him their drafts. 'Not editorial control,' he said, 'just for fact-checking.' I saw one of these drafts because Ben brought it with him to one of our sessions. It was a gracefully written tribute.

Ben never broke down in these sessions, though there were many times when his eyes reddened and his voice wobbled.

For my part, I reminded myself that I could not be helpful to Ben if I became overwhelmed by the emotion of hearing such an intensely felt account of a life that was swiftly winding down. I arranged some sessions with a fellow coach where I could express some of my feelings as well as my concerns about how well or not I was doing this work, though even in these conversations I did not give way to tears.

It came to our sixth session.

'You remember that meditation you did with us? Like a lot of others, I found it great, despite all my jokes about how we scientists don't do woo-woo stuff and that was woo-woo stuff all right.'

'What was it you liked?'

'The incredible feeling of peace and confidence I experienced. I'd like to do it again.'

Ben had one further request. I do this work from my apartment. It has no traffic noise and faces water. It is airy and open
plan, has light from three sides and an abundance of leafy green-
ery on the terraces. Clients and I sit in comfortably padded
armchairs around a small table. Ben pointed at the other side of
the room, away from the place where we normally worked. 'My
special request is that I'd like to lie on that couch so that this time
I can close my eyes and savour the whole thing properly. You can
channel Dr Freud and sit behind me.'

In the last years of his life, and living in that house in London,
Freud stoically endured surgeries and radiotherapy for cancer
of the jaw, refusing even the mildest painkiller lest it cloud his
mind. He seems to have approached his death with equanimity,
satisfied that his life's work was complete.

Ben was not to know the special significance this piece of
furniture has for me. Technically, it is a chaise longue or day-
bed and is of much the same vintage as the one in Freud's
room. It was probably bought by my grandmother when she
was a newly married young woman. The marriage was not
happy. Her son, my father, came to dislike her and what he
called her 'histrionics', but I loved her. I found her stylish, dramatic and interesting, a daring contrast to the suburban dreari-
ness I saw all around me. To me, she was always secretly a
glamorous figure. Later I realized she had been hopelessly
trapped in the conventions of her time when her considerable musical gifts could not find expression and when there
was no escape from a miserable marriage. She had listened
to me patiently and allowed me to sprawl all over that chaise
longue while I tried on her jewellery and told her some of my
childish secrets and worries. I begged to claim this piece of
furniture after her death, despite my father's scorn for its 'old-
fashionedness' and the further problem of having no home in
which to house it at the time. It has been renovated and recovered countless times, especially after its plump sides have

proved irresistible to the claws of generations of cats. It is the only thing I own that belonged to my grandmother.

We did the meditation. I ask the client to choose the time period at which they see their future self, aware as I explained these simple 'rules' to Ben that 'future' had its own strictures for him. Some clients prefer to keep the experience private, some like to describe it. I wait for them to tell me if they wish – or not.

Ben opened his eyes slowly, gave a little stretch and stood up calmly. 'Yes, that did it for me. You know what? My future self just turned around, smiled, beckoned, said a few words, waved and walked slowly away from me, into that lovely orange grove that I imagined at dusk, the one I remember from a fantastic holiday in Sicily. He just faded from sight. Very tranquil, just right.'

I have guided clients through this visualization many times and this is the only one as far as I know where the 'future self' has walked away.

That was it. Our programme was over.

Even when someone's death is expected, it is still a shock to learn of it. Scrolling through the newspaper on my iPad, I came to Ben's obituary, read words which I had already seen several months previously and heard myself give the involuntary ex-clamation, 'Oh no!' I read again of his many achievements as a scientist, his kindness and generosity as a teacher and mentor, then of the way he had continued working until the very last month of his life. I read of his devotion to his family and the peacefulness of his death.

I was proud to be invited to a memorial event for Ben, resolutely non-religious and held in a venue big enough to accommodate the many who attended. His colleagues had created a touching video tribute. It included some home movies, snatches of for-mal presentations at conferences and some speeches. The last sequence was of a dinner where Ben had officially handed over the presidency of a particular body to a colleague. As I heard him say the words on the video, 'And now it's time for me to move on,' I felt overwhelmed with a profound sense of loss and, for the first time, found myself in tears. The complete stranger sitting next to me quietly gripped my hand.

The sudden diagnosis of a terminal illness is a trauma in itself. It can be exactly like the experience of being caught up in a terrible accident, losing your job with cruel suddenness, being betrayed by a partner you loved and trusted. Everything you have assumed about the world is turned upside down. You have believed that behaving well will be rewarded by good things happening to you. You have assumed that bad things only happen to bad people. To discover that bad things can happen to good people can be horrifying. Recovery lies in the belief that you can still make choices, for instance about how you react to whatever the traumatic event has been.

Ben and I had discussed this many times, sharing an abiding admiration for Viktor Frankl's book *Man's Search for Meaning*. Frankl was a doctor imprisoned at Auschwitz during the Second World War, cold, hungry, ill, surrounded by dead and dying people. Despite being at daily risk of being murdered, he still found the resourcefulness to decide that no one could remove his ability to make choices about how he responded. Frankl believed that as long as you have a purpose in life you can survive anything and after the war he founded a thriving school of psychotherapy devoted to this concept. I have his book always available on my iPad. Ben and I read some favourite passages to each other, including this one:

The way in which a man accepts his fate and all the suffering it entails, the way in which he takes up his cross, gives him ample opportunity – even under the most difficult circumstances – to add a deeper meaning to his life. It may remain brave, dignified and unselfish. Or in the bitter fight for self-preservation he may forget his human dignity and become no more than an animal. Here lies the chance for a man either to make use of or to forgo the opportunities of attaining the moral values that a difficult situation may afford him. And this decides whether he is worthy of his sufferings or not.

We fool ourselves if we think that tears at a funeral or memorial event are exclusively about the lost person. They are more likely to be a reminder of our own mortality, and in this case, about the importance of dying well. I looked at the ashen faces of Ben's children bravely managing their tears and felt certain that the gift of having had such a father would flow through their lives. I thought of my own newest little grandchild, hoping that I could assure myself of something similar as I face the last part of my own life. I thought about my luck in having a career where age is an advantage of sorts, which allows me the freedom to do the work I love and which does not depend on physical capacity. As ever, if you are open to it as a coach, you can learn as much, sometimes more, from your client as your client can learn from you.

Recently I was running a workshop for a group of new coaches. The topic was that misty borderland between coaching and psychotherapy, and I briefly described my work with Ben.

We discussed the lazy labelling that is involved in saying that people do or do not have emotional intelligence or are allegedly 'on the [autistic] spectrum' and how easy it is to confuse reticence with lack of emotional intelligence. What greater test of emotional intelligence can there be than to manage the ending of your life with calm and humour?

Some of these coaches were troubled. The newer a coach is to coaching, the more frightened they tend to be about 'being in over your head', 'causing harm', or 'pretending to be a therapist when you're not'.

'Wasn't this a classic example of someone who needed therapy or counselling and not coaching?' one of them asked.

I explained how Ben and I had negotiated this topic, adding, 'But this was actually a classic piece of coaching. Ben never lost belief in his ability to make choices. The effect may have been therapeutic, and I hope and believe that it was, but it was not therapy. The client brought his goal, he wanted to be coached through his options; we did that. The fact that it was about preparing for the end of his life gave it a tremendously serious quality, though we did often laugh together as well. And yes, of course it was "life coaching".'

'Did you ever find out what the future self said to him in that meditation?' asked another.

'Yes,' I replied. 'It was, "You can choose fearlessness and I promise that you can and will have a good death."'

Time Spent With a Cat is Never Wasted

'I have a baffling case for you.'

It was Josh, a headteacher who had attended one of my courses.

As coaching has become more familiar, it has spread into many professions. It has become obvious that it offers a more productive and respectful way of managing people than the old top-down command-and-control philosophy because it trusts people to be able to make sound decisions for themselves. It has proved its value for every kind of manager.

It fits particularly well with the essential purposes of education. The headteachers who come on our courses grasp the principles quickly and are eager to apply them. Often they are executive heads, meaning that they are running several schools in ever more complex operations, not just making sure the children are happy and motivated but that the weighty inspection regime of targets and paperwork demanded by the government is kept in unobtrusive order.

Josh confessed himself stumped.

'Agneta is one of our teachers from Eastern Europe,' he said. 'She's a maths specialist and we were so pleased to find her, especially as we'd had this vacancy for nearly a year. But something is wrong and I've used all my coaching wiles to try to find out what it is and I've got nowhere.'

Josh described Agneta as finding it challenging to make the transition from the more formal style of teaching familiar in her home country.

'I think in her previous schools, the teachers stand in front of a class sitting in rows. That's so different from the informal way we do it, with children working in little groups.'

He went on, 'Agneta is tremendously polite and says she's grateful for all the attention we're giving her. This includes, by the way, giving her a mentor to observe her lessons, but she seems withdrawn and I don't know what's going on. I've chatted with her and asked her what else is happening in her life that it might help to know about, but she just shakes her head. She's so formal, always polite, rarely smiles – she's unnecessarily deferential to me. I don't want to lose her. I think she's got the makings of a very good member of the team. I apologize for this. You can guess what I'm about to say. My budget is minute, but will you see her for maybe three sessions at your most merciful rate? I've discussed it with her, she's definitely up for it, and she knows that it won't be about the technicalities of teaching.'

I heard a cheeky smile in Josh's voice as he went on. 'I've bigged you up to her. Told her that because of your experience and your books you're an expert on coaching. So how could she say no?'

'Josh,' I said, 'I will forgive that. Flattery will get you three pro bono sessions for Agneta and if she needs more after that we can talk budget.'

Soon I was exchanging emails with Agneta. Her first to me began, 'Dear Professor Rogers'.

'I'm not a professor,' I wrote in my reply. 'Coaching is very informal. Please call me Jenny.' Nonetheless, when I opened the door to her for our first session, she shook hands gravely, bowed slightly and said, 'I am honoured to meet you, Dr Rogers. I feel most privileged to have you as my coach.'

I said, 'Thank you, but I'm not any kind of doctor any more than I'm a professor, so if we are to work together please use my first name. Coaching is about working as equals and we can't do that if I call you by your first name – which I'd like to have permission to do – while you address me by a formal title.'

Agneta nodded but looked cautious. 'I'll try.'

I guessed that despite her scrupulously composed expression she was startled to be offered coffee and perhaps even more startled that I made it myself while she stood at the other side of my kitchen counter, a sturdy figure, formally dressed and with a boxy handbag looped over one arm. I wondered if she had thought we would be meeting in some kind of austere white space with a cluster of impressive diplomas on the walls, but here we were in my apartment with not a diploma to be seen.

We moved upstairs to the open area where I do the coaching. I pointed to the identical armchairs, carefully chosen to be a comfortable compromise between slouchy and upright. 'Choose your chair,' I said, 'there's no special significance in either one.'

In virtually all coaching engagements the agenda will already have been sketched out before the first session, even if only vaguely. This time it had not been, but I was content to see what would happen.

'So what would you like to see change as a result of this coaching?' I asked.

Agneta once again looked a little startled. 'I thought Mr – I mean Josh – would have told you . . .'

'All I know from Josh is what he said to me in a short phone call, and that wasn't much.' I relayed the hazy information Josh had supplied. 'He's concerned that things don't seem right for you and he sees coaching as a way of you – and me – exploring whatever the difficulties turn out to be.'

Success in coaching depends on having at least some clarity about goals. Unless you know what you are aiming for, how can you possibly know which direction the conversation should take or, in due course, review whether the coaching has worked? But sometimes the goals remain muddled, or just absent, and yet the client has made the effort to come to you and therefore probably has some need that they believe you could meet.

Silence. Agneta squeezed her lips together and looked at the floor.

'Let's leave that for the moment,' I said. 'Let's see how we go.'

I reminded Agneta of our email exchanges where I had described coaching as a process where you can review what's going well and what's going less well in your life, where you can look at the gap between how things are and how you'd like them to be, professionally and personally.

'The essential condition is that we both have to be real. This isn't a place for pretending. I will ask you every now and again how you think we're getting on. And you can say whatever you think will help you get what you want. There's no feedback from me to the school even though they've commissioned this work. It's an act of trust. I have to trust you to be honest and open with me, and you have to trust me to be honest and open with you – and to trust me to keep whatever you say confidential. If trust isn't there, nothing works.'

I paused. 'How does all of this strike you?'

'Trust, you say, and I think you may have used that word just now five times,' said Agneta slowly. 'That's hard for someone like me.'

'Trust is hard for you because . . .?'

Haltingly, Agneta told me she had been born in East Germany at the tail end of the communist regime to a German father and Polish mother. The collapse of the GDR in 1989 had been followed by a torrent of anger at the revelation that the secret police, the Stasi, seemed to have recruited one informant for every six people in the population, probably the most thorough and repressive attempt to control the thoughts and actions of its citizens of any state anywhere in the history of the world. From 1992 it had been possible for people to see exactly what files the Stasi had held on them.

'My father was one of those informers,' said Agneta. 'He had informed on workmates, on neighbours and even on my mother. Trust? He'd betrayed it, and even now, knowing what I know about how the Stasi operated through blackmail and coercion, I find it impossible to accept.'

Agneta's parents divorced. She and her mother moved to Poland. She never saw her father again.

'That sounds very, very difficult for you. A massive set of changes. Going to a new country, having to make new friends, different school, different language, not seeing your dad . . . What was the impact on you?'

Agneta told me calmly that she had 'coped'. She had adapted, accepted that her life in Germany had ended, had settled in to a new life.

'And that word *trust*?'

'Trust of any kind was difficult for me,' she said. 'My mother was a nurse. She took a job working nights in the local hospital, leaving me on my own, and then because she needed to sleep during the day I had to get myself to school even though I was only ten years old.'

'So you had to rely on yourself?'

'Yes, I suppose I felt that it was better to expect nothing from other people. Having a sense of control has always been important to me.'

Agneta had decided that teaching offered safety and predictability. As an outstanding student she had had no difficulty in getting the right university place. Mathematics was attractive because it was logical, there were right answers, it was dependable. Teaching? There would always be a need for teachers, so you would always have a job.

'It sounds as if you chose teaching because it was something you *could* do rather than because it was something you really *wanted* to do?'

Agneta shrugged. 'That's right. And it's turned out to be exactly as I expected. It's provided me with a living including making it possible to leave Poland with my daughter for a better life here.'

Agneta was aware that she had at least in part followed her mother's pattern. She had divorced her husband and brought her only child to live in a new country. 'Except,' she said, 'I've been a lot more careful about her welfare than my mother was able to be about mine. My daughter already spoke good English, now her English is perfect, she loves her school, she wants to stay here and so do I.'

We were about halfway through the session. Time to raise the question once more of why we were having this conversation at all.

'So what's the link between this and your experience at your current school?'

'They're wonderful people and they've made me welcome. But I think sometimes they don't always acknowledge that there's a case for a different approach to maths teaching.'

Sometimes as a coach, a client catches your interest with a topic that you and they find important. The conversation turns into the kind of discussion you might have at a conference with a fellow participant, but it is not coaching. I am deeply interested in teaching methodology because I have been some kind of a teacher all my life. The debate with Agneta was about so-called Shanghai mathematics teaching, a whole-class method that emphasizes rote learning, chanting and teacher-led interaction. It has been credited with the superior performance of Chinese children in mathematics. There is a great deal of controversy about it in the UK. It raises questions about how we learn, about how far learning should be teacher-dominated and about how we enable less gifted children to achieve. We had this discussion. Agneta remained as serious, as cool, as respectful as she had been throughout the session, without answering my questions: *What brings you here today? What is the work we need to be doing?*

I looked at my watch. Five minutes left. I asked her if there was a connection between her preferred teaching method and the issue of trust that she had emphasized as being so important to her. The question silenced her. I asked, more directly, what was the reason for the sense that she had become, in Josh's word, 'withdrawn'? Did Agneta want to introduce Shanghai methods to her British school? Did she believe that these methods were better?

She looked away. 'Something has shifted in my life, something has ended, something is over, and I don't know what to do to make it right again.'

I said, 'Agneta, I've enjoyed this conversation and I've been intrigued and touched by the story of your life. But all this feels very polite, very restrained, and only now in our last few minutes have I got any glimpse that there might be something bothering you that we could work with. How do you feel we are getting on?'

Agneta looked at me appraisingly. 'It's difficult for me. You say to trust you but how do I know I can?'

'You can't know, you can only take that leap of faith and judge by how you find me. People believe what we do, not what we say, so it's no good my just urging you to trust me. You'll have to make your own decision. How are you finding this experience of working with me so far?'

'You listen, um, er, nicely.'

'Nicely?'

'Yes. You seem to hear me but it's a little bit – what's the word? – intense for me.'

'What is it about intensity of listening that feels – what, alarming? Is that too strong a word?'

'Yes, alarming is right. It's about being seen, really seen . . .'

There was a pause while I reminded myself that so often the most important single thing in a session is said in the last few minutes.

'We've run out of time, unfortunately, but let's pick up this theme in our next session.'

As she left, Agneta shook my hand and gave another little bow. 'Thank you. This has been interesting.' I was aware that she still had not used my first name.

Interesting – that most bland of words.

Reflecting later about how I had allowed myself to be drawn into a theoretical discussion about teaching, I acknowledged that sometimes muddling along is the best you can hope for in a session. Most people find it rewarding to have the full attention of another human being who does not interrupt, interpret, judge or offer trite advice. For someone who knew all too well from her own history what it could mean to have personal scrutiny, was it possible that ordinary coaching questions could have echoes of interrogation? Had my scrupulously given attention seemed disturbing – or even invasive?

There was a long pause between the first session and the next. This was because in the interim I had elective surgery on both knees and knew that recovery would be lengthy. I suspended my work. Agneta was the first client I scheduled after this break. On the day itself I was having second thoughts about whether this was wise, having discovered that major surgery is treated by the body as a traumatic event regardless of whether you have 'elected' for it or not. There are unnerving effects on your mental as well as your physical health and, after the drama of the surgery, my progress felt plodding. For the first time in my life I was aware that I was experiencing either actual depression or something like it. The initial session with Agneta had felt like a failure; was I now just setting myself up for more of the same?

We began with the same solemn handshake. We moved upstairs as before, I considerably more slowly than Agneta, and this time she was carrying the tray of coffee. I began as I normally do by asking what reflections we might share of our first discussion. I was planning to express my regret at indulging myself with a theoretical discussion about teaching and my puzzlement at her reserve. I planned to enquire into her cryptic comment about what had ended in her life and to return to the theme of 'being seen', along with the threat that this might represent for her.

Before this could happen, Agneta's grave expression suddenly changed. She was breaking into a wide smile. She was laughing and giggling. I had my back to the stairwell so it took me a second or two to understand. My cat had padded silently up the stairs and was now heading purposefully for Agneta.

'Oh, he's so gorgeous and so funny! I've never seen a cat with such an amusing face!'

It's true that people did find this cat's face 'funny' with its unusual snub nose, round orange eyes, forward-curving whiskers, chubby cheeks and the white markings around his muzzle that suggest a comedy moustache. Now the cat was sizing up the distance between the floor and Agneta's lap.

'Oh dear,' I said, flapping my arms and making shooing-off gestures. 'He'll shed grey fur all over your skirt.'

'No, no!' she cried. 'He must jump up!' She patted her lap invitingly.

I need to explain my astonishment at this move.

I cannot imagine life without a cat. My previous cat was a tiny Persian adopted from a rescue centre. She was thirteen, entirely toothless, and her long fur was matted and filthy from neglect. She gave me three years of devoted affection before she died of kidney failure. Still mourning her loss, I had contacted the rescue centre again, thinking it unlikely they would immediately have a cat who needed what I offered: a quiet home but with no proper outside access other than the chance to roam the terraces of an apartment block. To my surprise, they said, 'We have just the cat for you: come straight away!'

This was another sorry tale: a four-year-old brown tabby, a Persian–British Shorthair cross. The family who had bought him from the breeder had most probably allowed their growing brood of children to pester him, dragging him about like a toy and shouting at him when it was evident how much he hated it. He had responded with what the rescue centre described as: 'The cat equivalent of a nervous breakdown – he just went to ground and hid. They had the sense in the end to bring him here.'

I had looked at this poor cat, whom I could see was large and handsome, desperately trying to be invisible, pressed wretchedly against the back wall of his pen. I decided immediately that I would adopt him. He had cowered under my bed for five days, refusing all food. It had taken a year of patient coaxing to get to the point where he had trusted me enough to sit on my lap and another year before he had stopped bolting to hide the moment he heard the door buzzer. Slowly, he made it clear that I was his person: he was never far away, affectionate and attentive. But he was still timid, still hypervigilant, wary of anyone new.

Now here was this cat doing something he had never once done before, leaping on to the lap of a total stranger, holding his chin up to be stroked.

'He's so adorable! What's his name?'

'His name,' I said, 'is Freddy.'

'It's *Freddy*? But . . . my middle name is Fryderyka after my grandmother, such an old-fashioned name! My closest friends call me Freddie. I see Agneta as the formal part of my life as well as the German part and since I left university I've never been called Agneta except at work!' Agneta looked like an entirely different person. She was smiling, she was laughing. Freddy stood proudly on her lap, kneading her skirt, giving full throttle to rattling purrs. At one point he craned up to give her (cat-haters, look away now) a tiny kiss on her nose, the ultimate in how cats express affection.

I had given Agneta some homework. This was to identify several times in her life when she had been 'in the zone', or 'in flow', the state of mind and body where we feel at our peak, we are doing something that matters, that is challenging, yet feels doable, that needs and uses all our skills. Self-doubt is banished and when whatever it is has been accomplished there is exhilaration and a feeling of profound, lasting satisfaction.

'Think about those events,' I had said. 'They could be projects, a whole period in a job or your personal life, or they could be something that only lasted a few minutes, it doesn't matter, but come prepared to talk them through with me next time.'

As an 'exercise', what this does is to identify deeply held values as well as revealing fundamental needs and motivators often with a direct relevance to career and life choices.

When I train coaches I am acutely aware of their potential love affair with what they call *tools and techniques*. With their wobbly confidence – and I was just the same as a beginner – people coming fresh to being a coach can feel that as long as you use some kind of technique with a client, the necessary change will happen and you will be doing your job. You believe that the technique will do the work. Decades as a coach have taught me that success in coaching is nothing to do with techniques. The only thing that matters is creating an authentic connection. But exactly how and why this works mystifies me now as much as it did when it was all brand new. Clients constantly astonish me by finding what they need from a session in ways I could not possibly have imagined or foreseen.

Asking Agneta to identify the experience of being 'in flow' was one such technique, but the energy of her response was largely the result of her unexpected encounter with my cat.

She cuddled and stroked her namesake on her lap. For the first time she talked with animation. All her many stories of being 'in the zone' were about organizing ambitious events. She had run a successful fundraising Coin Trail around the school, working enthusiastically with parents and staff. She had raised money to give holidays to refugee children from Syria. She had decluttered and then thoroughly cleaned a friend's house as a birthday gift. She had loved the thrills involved in the year-long eBay trading that had financed her determination to leave Poland. Not one of her tales involved mathematics or teaching. We discussed the implications. Agneta's moments of delight, fulfilment and satisfying skill had nothing whatsoever to do with being a maths teacher and everything to do with being an entrepreneurial organizer.

'And,' I said, 'what also comes out of this discussion is your strong commitment to social justice. Is that right?'

It was right. 'It's easy in London,' she said, 'with such an integrated Polish community from three generations ago, to forget how many newly arrived East Europeans are now living on the margins with so little money. Have you noticed, for instance, that on your canal towpath, a bit further on from your flat, there is that little group of men – have you seen them? I knew straight away they were Polish. I stopped to talk to them. They wear work boots and yellow bibs and they're standing about chatting but they're not just taking a break from work. They don't have work and they're all sleeping rough!' I heard the passion and indignation in her voice. 'So many worries about visas, about Brexit, about accommodation, about prejudice. I've seen how fear affects people – I want to do something about it and I think I could!'

Agneta turned to her feelings about her colleagues. 'They're so admirable and amazing,' she said. 'They really do trust the children to want to learn, they are graceful and funny and creative and confident in their skills. It has been so impressive to see it and to realize that, however much mentoring I get, I will never be their equal. I don't have that inborn talent and I just can't find the motivation to acquire it. I feel guilty. I feel I came to the school on false pretences.'

Freddy gave a languorous yawn and clambered on to the back of Agneta's chair, stretching out so that his face and front paws were lightly hugging one side of her neck while his tail and one back leg hung elegantly down the other side. He looked like a living scarf. She occasionally reached up to tickle his chin again.

Towards the end of the session I was finding it increasingly hard to concentrate. My knees were aching from the now unfamiliar discipline of having been in one position for ninety minutes. I had the beginnings of a headache. I was slumping. I was aware of needing to simulate more interest than I was feeling. Maybe it had not been such a good idea to start work again so soon. All those people, including my sons, who had anxiously warned me about not rushing back to work had probably been right. As we were finishing and I was congratulating Agneta on her enthusiasm and clear-sightedness, she suddenly peered at me shrewdly and said, 'Jenny, you look tired.'

'That's the first time you've used my name!' I said, while stoutly denying that I was tired. 'Really, I'm fine.'

We made our way downstairs, she a lot more lithely than I.

As we did, I thought, *What am I saying? I've asked this client to be real and now I'm not being authentic myself.* I stopped halfway down the stairs and said, 'We made a commitment to be real and, to be honest, you're quite right. I am tired. I'm glad I can go and have a nap now. It's taking me much longer than I ever dreamt to get all my energy back after surgery.'

'Yes, I thought so,' said Agneta, smiling calmly.

It came to our third and final session. Even though I had anticipated it, I could hardly believe the change. Agneta was lively, jokey, eager.

'Where's my Freddy?' she cried as we made our way to the coaching area. But he had heard her and was already trotting up the stairs, ready to leap on to her lap once more.

We discussed Agneta's plans. These were to inform Josh that she had realized teaching was not for her. This meant teaching of every style, formal or informal. She would tell him that she would stay until the end of the summer term and help recruit a successor if he wished. After that she would be fulfilling a long-standing ambition to run her own business. This business would be a house-cleaning service which would come and blitz your home, decluttering first if necessary. I was interested in the idea. A year previously I had employed just such a company. Four anxious-looking Romanian women were delivered by van at eight in the morning and worked tirelessly, speaking to each other rarely, with no break whatsoever despite my offers of refreshments, until four in the afternoon. Then the same anonymous van came to collect them. Most of our communication was in sign language. The words 'modern slavery' kept coming uneasily into my head. The work they did was impeccably thorough but my thought was 'never again'.

Agneta agreed. She knew several such companies and strongly disapproved of them. She would use her many contacts to recruit, train and cherish her staff. She would provide ample opportunities for them to learn English and to move on if they wished. They would be properly employed rather than being workers in the gig economy. She would create a climate that was open and generous. Her prices would be higher, but her customers would get cheerful, skilled, committed, articulate people and in all probability would come back for more. In the meantime, she was applying for British citizenship for herself and her daughter as a safeguard against what she called 'Brexit Churn' and as recognition that her future life was in the UK. A woman who had already endured one change of country and language as a child, then another as an adult, was preparing to make yet another valiant change.

Change in midlife is never as simple as it may look from the outside. For every beginning there is an ending. For every gain there is a loss. For every 'yes' there is a 'no'. It takes bravery to give up the familiar, even when the familiar feels like a prison. You will disappoint or worry some of the people in your life. You will question whether what you are planning is the right path. You will experience disappointment and blind alleys. You will doubt whether you have the skill and resilience to survive in a new life. The risks may be substantial. For all these reasons I encourage clients to take their time, but it was clear to me that

Agneta was ready. The hesitations had already been expressed in the 'withdrawn' behaviour that Josh had described.

Agneta gave Freddy a final stroking behind his ears before tipping him gently from her lap.

A few months later, thankfully feeling far better about my physical and mental state, I had an email from Freddie, as she had now urged me to call her. The subject line was 'Time spent with a cat is never wasted'. The email said:

> *Droga Jenny, nie Pani Doktor, nie Pani Profesor (these are Polish words by the way, in case you're wondering, for 'Dear Jenny, not Madam Doctor, not Madam Professor'.)*
>
> *Greetings from the other Freddie in your life. I wanted to make you laugh with this quote, see above. Supposedly it was said by that French novelist Colette but I can't find where, so perhaps she never said it. But don't you think it's so true? Give the Amazing Freddy-Cat a big kiss from me and tell him he has magical cat powers that are a secret between him and me. Don't ask him about it because he won't say. I've told the school now; everyone is happy and all my plans are going ahead. I still wonder sometimes if I'm crazy, but I don't think so. My life as a teacher will be ending and this feels so right, it's time! This is to send a big thank you. My team will come and clean your apartment for zero money (just once!) so you can judge for yourself how good we are then you can recommend us to all your friends and clients – just ask, but not before September!!*
> *Freddie*
> *Xx*

For the record, Freddy the cat never repeated his flirtatious advances with anyone else. A year later he died aged thirteen after a sudden and mercifully short illness, a cat who will always have a place in my heart and I think in Freddie/Agneta's too.

Acknowledgements

I owe gratitude to the many people who helped me while this book was in its long gestation. Their support ranged from meticulous reading and re-reading, insightful feedback and specific suggestions on content or style, to friendship, hospitality, endless listening and cups of coffee or glasses of wine when most needed. My warmest thanks to you all: Helen Boaden; Jane Cook; Maria Farress; Maria Fay; Zelida Gordon, Monika Lee; Laura Longrigg; Jaime Marshall; Martina O'Sullivan; Dorota Porazka; Jo Prior; Oliver Rawlins; Charlie Rogers; Luke Rogers; Owen Rogers; Theo Farress Rogers; Nicholas Spice; Joe Treasure; Julia Vaughan Smith; Karen Whitlock and Leni Wildflower.

PENGUIN PARTNERSHIPS

Penguin Partnerships is the Creative Sales and Promotions team at Penguin Random House. We have a long history of working with clients on a wide variety of briefs, specializing in brand promotions, bespoke publishing and retail exclusives, plus corporate, entertainment and media partnerships.

We can respond quickly to briefs and specialize in repurposing books and content for sales promotions, for use as incentives and retail exclusives as well as creating content for new books in collaboration with our partners as part of branded book relationships.

Equally if you'd simply like to buy a bulk quantity of one of our existing books at a special discount, we can help with that too. Our books can make excellent corporate or employee gifts.

Special editions, including personalized covers, excerpts of existing books or books with corporate logos can be created in large quantities for special needs.

We can work within your budget to deliver whatever you want, however you want it.

For more information, please contact
salesenquiries@penguinrandomhouse.co.uk